This Book Comes With a Website

W9-AXT-268

Nolo's award-winning website has a page dedicated just to this book, where you can:

KEEP UP TO DATE – When there are important changes to the information in this book, we'll post updates

READ BLOGS – Get the latest info from Nolo authors' blogs

LISTEN TO PODCASTS – Listen to authors discuss timely issues on topics that interest you

WATCH VIDEOS – Get a quick introduction to a legal topic with our short videos

And that's not all. Nolo.com contains thousands of articles on everyday legal and business issues, plus a plain-English law dictionary, all written by Nolo experts and available for free. You'll also find more useful **books, software, online services,** and **downloadable forms.**

NOLO
LAW for ALL

Get updates and more at
www.nolo.com/back-of-book/PRAV.html

△△ NOLO **The Trusted Name**
(but don't take our word for it)

"In Nolo you can trust."
THE NEW YORK TIMES

"Nolo is always there in a jam as the nation's premier publisher of do-it-yourself legal books."
NEWSWEEK

"Nolo publications…guide people simply through the how, when, where and why of the law."
THE WASHINGTON POST

"[Nolo's]…material is developed by experienced attorneys who have a knack for making complicated material accessible."
LIBRARY JOURNAL

"When it comes to self-help legal stuff, nobody does a better job than Nolo…"
USA TODAY

"The most prominent U.S. publisher of self-help legal aids."
TIME MAGAZINE

"Nolo is a pioneer in both consumer and business self-help books and software."
LOS ANGELES TIMES

10th Edition

8 Ways to
Avoid Probate

Mary Randolph, J.D.

TENTH EDITION   APRIL 2014

Cover Design   SUSAN PUTNEY

Book Design   TERRI HEARSH

Proofreading   SUSAN CARLSON GREENE

Index   BAYSIDE INDEXING SERVICES

Printing   BANG PRINTING

ISSN: 1931-0889 (print)

ISSN: 2332-7049 (online)

ISBN: 978-1-4133-2014-5 (pbk)

ISBN: 978-1-4133-2015-2 (epub ebook)

This book covers only United States law, unless it specifically states otherwise.

Please note

We believe accurate, plain-English legal information should help you solve many of your own legal problems. But this text is not a substitute for personalized advice from a knowledgeable lawyer. If you want the help of a trained professional—and we'll always point out situations in which we think that's a good idea—consult an attorney licensed to practice in your state.

Acknowledgments

My heartfelt thanks go to:

Jake Warner, who, as always, provided enthusiasm, support, and spot-on editing.

Denis Clifford, who gave generous and valuable help reviewing the manuscript. I am also indebted to him for the wealth of information in his own estate planning books.

Naomi Starkman, who cheerfully and doggedly helped with legal research for the first edition, and Ella Hirst, who carefully updated statutory references for several subsequent editions.

Two Nolo authors, Twila Slesnick, Ph.D., a tax and retirement specialist who provided clear answers on murky retirement plan issues; and Tony Mancuso, who provided up-to-the-minute information on small business law.

My colleagues and friends at Nolo, who make coming to work a genuine pleasure.

My family, who supply the love and support that make everything else possible.

About the Author

Mary Randolph gave up the practice of law to write and edit Nolo books and software and has never regretted it for a minute. She received her law degree from Boalt Hall, the law school at the University of California at Berkeley. She is the author of Nolo materials on living trusts, *Deeds for California Real Estate,* and *The Executor's Guide: Settling a Loved One's Estate or Trust,* also published by Nolo. She lives in the San Francisco Bay Area.

Table of Contents

I Introduction: Thinking About Probate Avoidance..........1

Is It Worth Your While to Avoid Probate?.....................2

What Probate Avoidance Can't Change..........................7

Comparing Probate-Avoidance Methods.......................11

A Lick of Common Sense..13

1 Set Up Payable-On-Death Accounts...........................15

The Paperwork...17

Adding a POD Designation to a Joint Account................19

Choosing Beneficiaries...21

If a Beneficiary Dies Before You Do...........................30

If You Change Your Mind.......................................32

Claiming the Money...34

2 Name a Beneficiary for Your Retirement Accounts.......37

Choosing a Beneficiary..39

Required Distributions From Retirement Accounts............52

3 Name a Beneficiary for Your Stocks and Bonds............57

Transfer-on-Death Registration.................................58

Registration of Government Bonds and Notes..................67

4 Name a Beneficiary for Your Vehicles.........................71

Transfer-on-Death Registration.................................72

Joint Ownership With the Right of Survivorship...............75

Special Transfer Procedures for Vehicles.......................77

5   Name a Beneficiary for Your Real Estate 81

Can You Use a TOD Deed? 82

How It Works: An Overview 83

Possible Drawbacks of TOD Deeds 85

How to Prepare, Sign, and Record the Deed 86

Three Ways to Cancel the Deed—And One Way Not To 90

How the New Owner Claims the Property 92

6   Hold Property In Joint Ownership 95

Kinds of Joint Ownership That Avoid Probate 96

Joint Tenancy 98

Tenancy by the Entirety 110

Community Property 112

Alternatives to Joint Ownership 122

7   Create a Living Trust 123

How a Living Trust Avoids Probate 126

Other Advantages of a Living Trust 130

Why You Still Need a Will 133

Do You Really Need a Living Trust? 134

Creating a Valid Living Trust 137

What Property to Put in a Trust 145

Taxes and Record Keeping 152

Amending or Revoking a Living Trust Document 153

8   Take Advantage of Special Procedures for Small Estates 155

Why Even Large Estates May Qualify 157

Claiming Wages With an Affidavit 160

Claiming Other Property With Affidavits 162

Simplified Court Procedures 166

9 Make Gifts..171

The Federal Gift Tax 173

Making Tax-Free Gifts..174

Gifts That Could Land You in Tax Trouble...179

What to Give 181

Gifts to Children..183

Thinking Before You Give 186

10 Putting It All Together...189

Alice and Frank: A Simple Life...190

Maria: Dealing With Widowhood..192

Mike: Midlife Concerns...196

Jim and Terry: An Unmarried Couple 198

Esther and Mark: New Love, Old Money 201

Linda and Tomas: Comfortable 204

G Glossary...207

A Appendix—State Information..219

I Index..273

Thinking About Probate Avoidance

Is It Worth Your While to Avoid Probate? 2

What Probate Avoidance Can't Change 7

    Taxes 7

    Your Family's Right to Inherit 7

    Your Creditors' Rights 9

Comparing Probate-Avoidance Methods 11

A Lick of Common Sense 13

Get Updates and More Online

When there are important changes to the information in this book, we'll post updates online, on a page dedicated to this book:

www.nolo.com/back-of-book/PRAV.html

You'll find other useful information there, too, including author blogs, podcasts, and videos.

Probate, lawyers say, is simply a safeguard, designed to ensure that your wishes are honored and your family protected when you are no longer around to oversee matters yourself. An impartial court supervises the whole process, to look out for the interests of both your family and your creditors. What's wrong with that?

A lot, unfortunately.

An Overview of Probate

During probate proceedings, a deceased person's will is brought to the local court. Proof must be shown that the will is authentic and was properly signed, with all the formalities required by state law. (If there is no valid will, the court determines who, under state law, stands to inherit the deceased's property.) The deceased person's property is inventoried and appraised, relatives and creditors are notified, and a notice is published in the local newspaper. Creditors make their claims, and debts are paid. Eventually—commonly, about a year later—the remaining property is distributed to the inheritors.

Is It Worth Your While to Avoid Probate?

Probate's problems have been well documented and well publicized. And if you've experienced the probate process firsthand, after the death of a parent or spouse, you probably don't need any convincing that avoidance is the best strategy. But in case you still aren't sure why planning to avoid probate is worth some effort, here are some factors to consider.

Where you live makes a big difference. Some states have adopted a law called the Uniform Probate Code, which simplifies probate court proceedings. In these states (check the appendix to see whether yours is among them), probate is likely to be simpler, quicker, and cheaper than in states that cling to the old-fashioned ways. The whole process is just paperwork, with no court hearings. Some other states have also simplified their probate court procedures.

Your family situation makes a difference. Probate usually entails notifying the deceased person's heirs—that is, the people who would have a legal claim to inherit if there were no will. (This is true even if the person *does* leave a valid will.) That's usually not a problem if there's a surviving spouse or children, because they would inherit everything under state law. But if the deceased person was elderly and didn't leave a spouse or any direct descendents, it can be an unexpected headache to try to locate heirs. The executor may have to track down long-lost aunts and uncles and their offspring—people no one in the family may have heard from in many years.

Probate is a waste of money. The cost of probate varies widely from state to state, but it's commonly estimated that probate attorney, court, and other fees can eat up as much as 5% of the value of property left behind at death. As a result, that much less goes to the people or charities you wanted to get it. If the estate is complicated or disputed, the fees can be even larger.

Probate Fees	
If you die with this much...	probate may cost up to this much...
$200,000	$10,000
$400,000	$20,000

Probate's cost might be justified if the process really did something for families. But in most instances, there is no conflict, so there's no need to be in court.

For example, say a man leaves a will that gives everything to his widow and children, as is common. No one is challenging the validity of the will, and the family is perfectly willing to pay whatever bills he left and divide up the property according to his wishes. Why have a lengthy court proceeding, formal notification of relatives and creditors, and expensive publication of death notices in the "legal notices" column of a newspaper? The property merely needs to be handed over to the new owners, which is what probate-avoidance methods let you do. The successful use of living trusts and other probate avoidance techniques by millions of Americans is convincing evidence that if probate were gone, we wouldn't miss it.

Lawyers' fees, set by statute or local custom, often bear no relation to actual work done. Courts are supposed to keep an eye on fees, but in practice, they very seldom intervene. And lawyers are almost always paid first—before the beneficiaries.

Some people slog through probate without hiring a lawyer, but in most states the system does little to encourage them. Just finding the right court can be a challenge. Depending on where you live, your will may be headed for Surrogate's Court, Orphans' Court, Circuit Court, Superior Court, or Chancery Court. Encouragingly, more probate courts are now putting good information and forms on their websites. And in a few states, good do-it-yourself materials are available; for example, Nolo publishes *How to Probate an Estate in California*, by Julia Nissley.

Probate takes too long. It depends on where you live and what you own, but it's not uncommon for probate to take a year, during which time the beneficiaries generally get nothing unless the judge allows the immediate family a "family allowance." In some states, this allowance is a pittance, only a few hundred dollars. In others, it can amount to thousands. In any case, the family is forced to ask a court for use of its own money—a demeaning and absurd situation.

Delay can be more than an annoyance; it can cause major life disruptions. A student about to enter college may not be able to if a parent's assets are tied up in probate for months or years. A surviving spouse may not be able to move to take a new job. And it's especially hard to run—or sell—a small business with the court looking over your shoulder.

Probate is public. Few people ever stop to think that a will—a very personal document, which may reveal much about both financial and family circumstances—becomes a matter of public record after its writer dies. Like all other probate documents, wills are examined and filed, and can be inspected by anyone who goes to the courthouse and asks.

If you're rich or famous, you can count on public scrutiny. In any bookstore, you can find books of nothing but the wills of famous people; Michael Jackson's will popped up on the Internet almost instantly after it was filed in court. Obviously, few people generate intense public interest—but if you're well known in your community, reporters may sniff around just to see if there's anything they consider newsworthy. And con artists have been known to use public records to gather information about surviving family members who might be vulnerable to scams.

If, on the other hand, you arrange for your property to pass outside of probate—via a living trust or payable-on-death bank account, for example—the transaction is private. No documents are filed with a court or any other government entity; what you leave to whom remains private. (There is one exception: Records of real estate ownership are always public.)

Each state requires a court proceeding. The only thing worse than regular probate is out-of-state probate. Usually, probate takes place in the county where the deceased person was living. But if there's real estate in another state, it's usually necessary to have a whole separate probate proceeding there, too. That means finding a lawyer in each state and financing multiple probate proceedings. No fun there.

Why Reform Doesn't Happen

If the probate system is such a mess, why hasn't it been cleaned up? It's the responsibility of state legislatures to change probate laws, and there have been some attempts at reform. But it's hardly a hot-button issue—no politician is going to get elected on a probate reform platform.

Some strides have been made, though. Many states have simplified their probate systems. And almost every state now has a streamlined probate procedure for "small estates." (See Chapter 8.)

Still, if the probate system were really gutted, it would threaten well-established interests. Probate lawyers, of course, stand to lose large amounts of easy money. Probate is a profit center for lawyers. That's why lawyers usually charge so much less for wills than they do for other documents of comparable complexity: They are hoping to cash in later, when the will must be probated.

A lawyer who accepts a probate case is almost guaranteed a nice profit for very little effort. Generally, probate entails lots of tedious paperwork but little or no original thinking. Most of the actual work is done by paralegals. There are few court appearances, if any, and very rarely is a lawyer called on to craft a legal argument or conduct anything resembling a trial.

Other industries milk the probate system as well: newspapers that publish the legal notices required in probate and businesses that sell the bonds executors must post, for example. Lobbyists for all these interests come out in force when proposed legislation would seriously cut into their profits.

The dearth of reform has, ultimately, spurred an end-run around probate. If you can't change it, people have decided, avoid it altogether.

What Probate Avoidance Can't Change

Avoiding probate has much to recommend it, as discussed above. But at the same time, it's not a magic bullet that solves every financial problem that might surface after your death. To clear up some common misconceptions, here are a few things that probate-avoidance has absolutely no effect on.

Taxes

Avoiding probate doesn't mean avoiding taxes. In fact, the two are completely unrelated. If you give away a lot of money during your life, or leave a lot at your death, the state and federal governments may take a chunk of it in the form of gift or estate tax. The government is uninterested in whether or not the property goes through probate court on its way to the people who inherit it.

Most people don't even need to think about federal gift and estate taxes. These taxes affect only people who make very large amounts of taxable gifts during life or leave very large estates at death. State taxes, however, may affect smaller estates. (Chapter 9 explains estate taxes.)

Your Family's Right to Inherit

If you're married, your spouse has a right to some of the property you leave at your death, and using probate-avoidance techniques to transfer the property doesn't change that. This, of course, is no problem for most people; most of us want very much to pass on to our spouses and children whatever wealth we've accumulated. In case you're concerned about this issue, however, here are the general rules regarding your family's rights.

Your spouse. Most married people leave much, if not all, of their property to their spouses. But if you don't, your spouse may have the right to go to court and claim some of your property after your death.

The rights of spouses vary from state to state. In the community property states (Arizona, California, Idaho, Louisiana, Nevada, New Mexico, Texas, Washington, and Wisconsin), the general rule is that spouses together own all property that either acquires during the marriage, except property one spouse receives by gift or inheritance. Each spouse owns a half-interest in this "community property." You are free to leave your separate property and your half of the community property to anyone you choose.

In most other states, a surviving spouse who doesn't receive at least one-third to one-half of the deceased spouse's property (through a will, a living trust, or another method) is entitled to insist upon that much. The exact share depends on state law. In short, a spouse who doesn't receive the minimum he or she is entitled to under state law (the "statutory share") may be entitled to some of the property in your living trust.

CAUTION

Don't try to cut out your spouse. If you don't plan to leave at least half of the property in your estate to your spouse, you should consult a lawyer experienced in estate planning.

State law may also give your spouse the right to inherit the family residence, or at least use it for his or her life. The Florida constitution, for example, gives a surviving spouse the family residence. (Fla. Const. Art. 10, § 4.) The spouse is free, of course, to voluntarily give up this right.

RESOURCE

More information. *Plan Your Estate*, by Denis Clifford (Nolo), contains a state-by-state list of surviving spouses' rights.

Children. Although most children inherit the bulk of their parents' property, usually after both parents have died, it isn't mandated by law. Put bluntly, you don't have to leave your children a dime. (The only exception is Louisiana, which has inheritance laws that are very different from all other states. This book doesn't cover Louisiana law.)

The law protects only children who appear to have been accidentally overlooked—typically, children born after the parent's will is signed. Such children are entitled to a share (the size is determined by state law) of the deceased parent's estate, which may include property in a living trust.

So if you don't want to leave any property to one or more of your children—perhaps they already have plenty of money, or you've already given them their inheritances—just make a will and mention each child in it. And to avoid any later misunderstandings or hurt feelings, explain your actions to your children, either in your will or—better—now, in person.

Grandchildren have no right to inherit from their grandparents unless their parent has died. In that case, the grandchildren essentially take the place of the deceased child and are entitled to whatever he or she would have been legally entitled to, if anything.

Your Creditors' Rights

Avoiding probate doesn't let you off the hook from legal obligations to your creditors. If you don't leave enough other assets to pay your debts and taxes, any assets that passed outside of probate may be subject to the claims of creditors after your death.

If there is any probate proceeding, your executor (the person named in your will to handle your affairs after your death) can demand that whoever inherited the property turn over some or all of it so that creditors can be paid. Creditors, however, have only a set amount of time—about three to six months, in most states—to submit formal claims to your executor. A creditor who is properly notified of the probate court proceeding cannot file a claim after the deadline passes.

On the other hand, when property isn't probated, creditors' claims aren't cut off so quickly. In theory, at least, a creditor could track down the property and sue the new owner to collect the debt a year or two later.

> **EXAMPLE:** Elaine is a real estate investor with a good-sized portfolio of property. At any one time she has many creditors, and she has even been sued once or twice. It might be to her advantage to have assets transferred by a probate court procedure, which requires creditors who are properly notified of the probate proceeding to file their claims promptly.

As a practical matter, however, avoiding probate may actually provide more protection from creditors. When property is distributed without probate, there is no legal requirement (as there is in probate) that creditors be notified in writing. They may not know of the death for years. They may not know where the property went, and especially if the debt is small, it may not be worth their while to track down the new owners and try to collect.

Most people don't need to worry that after their death, creditors will line up to collect large debts from the estate. In most situations, the surviving relatives simply pay the valid debts, such as monthly bills, taxes, and medical and funeral expenses. But if you are concerned about the possibility of large claims, you may want to let your property go through probate.

CAUTION
It's all or nothing. If you want to take advantage of probate's creditor cutoff, you must let all your property pass through probate. If not, the creditor could still sue (even after the probate claim deadline) and try to collect from the property that didn't go through probate.

Comparing Probate-Avoidance Methods

Given the plentiful drawbacks of probate, it's not surprising that people have sought ways around it. In a nutshell, you can avoid probate by using other documents in place of a will or by transferring property before your death.

Forty years ago, almost the only way to avoid probate was by using a trust. New methods have come along as part of new, government-created types of investments, such as private retirement accounts. People have eagerly taken up each new probate-avoidance method. In fact, as much property now passes to the next generation through nonprobate transfers as goes through probate, according to legal experts.

This book discusses common and straightforward ways to avoid probate. (And despite its title, it now discusses *nine* ways to avoid probate—a chapter on how to use transfer-on-death deeds was added when more and more states began allowing this important probate-avoidance method.) None of these methods requires hiring a lawyer; all involve very little or no expense.

Keep in mind that you can mix and match methods when you're planning to avoid probate. You may well want to use one technique for avoiding probate of real estate and another for stocks, for example. Some options for common kinds of assets are listed below. Not every option is available in every state; each method's advantages and limitations are discussed in detail later in the book.

Choosing the Right Probate-Avoidance Method	
Asset	**What You Can Do to Avoid Probate**
Real estate	• Transfer to a living trust • Hold property in joint tenancy with a co-owner or tenancy by the entirety with your spouse • Hold as community property (or community property with right of survivorship) with your spouse • Prepare a transfer-on-death deed
Bank accounts, certificates of deposit	• Name a payable-on-death beneficiary • Hold in joint tenancy with a co-owner or tenancy by the entirety with your spouse • Hold as community property (or community property with right of survivorship) with your spouse • Transfer to a living trust
Stocks and bonds	• Name a transfer-on-death beneficiary • Transfer to a living trust • Hold in joint tenancy with a co-owner or tenancy by the entirety with your spouse • Hold as community property (or community property with right of survivorship) with your spouse
Government bonds	• Register ownership in beneficiary form • Hold in joint tenancy with a co-owner or tenancy by the entirety with your spouse • Hold as community property (or community property with right of survivorship) with your spouse • Transfer to a living trust

Choosing the Right Probate-Avoidance Method, continued	
Asset	What You Can Do to Avoid Probate
Cars and other vehicles	• Register in transfer-on-death form • Hold in joint tenancy with a co-owner or tenancy by the entirety with your spouse • Hold as community property (or community property with right of survivorship) with your spouse • Transfer to a living trust
Retirement accounts (IRAs, 401(k) plans)	• Name a beneficiary to inherit at your death

Not all of these probate-avoidance methods are available in every state, and not all are appropriate in every situation. The chapters on each method explain their restrictions, advantages, and disadvantages.

A Lick of Common Sense

Probate avoidance is not a religion—or at least, it shouldn't be. To hear some people, though (especially the ones selling various probate-avoidance advice or documents), failing to avoid probate for every one of your assets is tantamount to neglecting a moral duty to your family.

Don't believe it. Doing some planning so that your family will be spared red tape and expense after your death is sensible and laudable, but keep in mind that probate doesn't happen until after your death. There's just no reason for a healthy 40-year-old to spend lots of time and effort to avert something that probably won't happen for many, many years. If you're young and healthy, a will, which lets you leave property to the people you choose and name someone you want to raise your children if you can't, is probably all the estate planning you need; you can worry about probate later. And even if you never do a bit of probate-avoidance planning, your family will endure some hassle and expense—but will survive.

In other words, use common sense. As you get older and decide it's worthwhile to do some probate-avoidance planning, keep in mind that your family will reap the most benefits if your big-ticket possessions, like real estate and large bank or investment accounts, don't go through probate. So take advantage of the simple, inexpensive methods outlined in this book to remove those assets from the probate system. But don't get carried away with trying to get every last teaspoon covered by a sure-fire probate-avoidance method.

If you're determined to devote that much energy to what will happen after your death, far better to spend some of it on things that really matter: the memories you will leave with loved ones, the difference you will have made in others' lives. After all, would you really want as your epitaph, "Didn't Spend a Nickel on Probate Fees"?

Set Up Payable-On-Death Accounts

The Paperwork... 17

Adding a POD Designation to a Joint Account 19

    Accounts With a Right of Survivorship.. 19

    Accounts With No Right of Survivorship.. 20

Choosing Beneficiaries 21

    Children 22

    Multiple Beneficiaries... 25

    Institutions or Businesses.. 27

    Your Spouse's Rights... 27

If a Beneficiary Dies Before You Do 30

If You Change Your Mind.. 32

    How to Change a POD Designation... 32

    Contradictory Will Provisions.. 33

    Property Settlement Agreements at Divorce 34

Claiming the Money... 34

Payable-on-death bank accounts offer one of the easiest ways to keep money—even large sums of it—out of probate. All you need to do is properly notify your bank of whom you want to inherit the money in the account or certificate of deposit. The bank and the beneficiary you name will do the rest, bypassing probate court entirely. It's that simple.

This kind of account has been called the "poor man's trust." The description is apt (if sexist) because a payable-on-death account does accomplish for a bank account—for free—exactly the same result as would an expensive, lawyer-drawn trust.

As long as you are alive, the person you named to inherit the money in a payable-on-death (POD) account has no rights to it. If you need the money, or just change your mind about leaving it to the beneficiary you named, you can spend the money, name a different beneficiary, or close the account.

Payable-on-Death Accounts at a Glance	
Pros	**Cons**
• They're easy to create. • There's no limit on how much money you can leave this way. • Designating a beneficiary for a bank account costs nothing. • It's easy for the beneficiary to claim the money after the original owner dies.	• You can't name an alternate beneficiary.

Payable-on-Death Account or "Totten Trust"?

Payable-on-death accounts go by different names in different states—and sometimes in the same state. Your bank, for example, may respond to your request for a payable-on-death account by handing you a form that authorizes the creation of something called a Totten trust. Payable-on-death bank accounts are also sometimes called tentative trusts, informal trusts, or revocable bank account trusts.

Totten trusts are really just payable-on-death accounts. The name comes from an old New York case (*Re Totten*), which was the first case to rule (in 1904) that someone could open a bank account as "trustee" for another person who had no rights to the money until the depositor died. Other courts had balked at this, objecting that such an account was tantamount to a will, which had to fulfill detailed legal requirements to be valid. The *Totten* court called the account a "tentative" (revocable) trust.

After this decision, courts in many other states adopted the idea of Totten trusts. Later, state legislatures enacted statutes authorizing payable-on-death accounts, specifically addressing many of the questions that had sprung up about Totten trusts. For example, some statutes state exactly how you can change a payable-on-death designation.

The Paperwork

Banks, savings and loans, and credit unions all offer payable-on-death accounts. They don't charge any extra fees for keeping your money this way. You can add a payable-on-death designation to any kind of new or existing account: checking, savings, or certificate of deposit.

Setting up a payable-on-death bank account is simple. When you open the account and fill out the bank's forms, just list the beneficiary on the signature card. The bank may also ask you for some other information, such as the beneficiary's address and birth date. (For example, the current address of each beneficiary is required by law in a few states.) The beneficiary of a payable-on-death account, who is commonly referred to as a "POD payee," doesn't have to sign anything.

> **EXAMPLE:** Magda wants to leave her two nieces some money. She opens a savings account at a local bank, deposits $10,000 in it, and names her two nieces as payable-on-death beneficiaries. After Magda's death ten years later, they claim the money in the account—including the interest paid by the bank—without going through probate.

If you choose an account that has restrictions on withdrawals—for example, a 24-month certificate of deposit—the early withdrawal penalty will probably be waived if you die before the period is up.

If you've considered changing a solely owned bank account to a joint account with the person you want to inherit the money after your death, you may be better off by simply naming the person as the POD beneficiary instead. There are several advantages.

If you added another person's name to yours on the account, that person would immediately have the right to withdraw money from the account. And, a creditor could come after his or her share of the account. (See Chapter 6.) A POD account avoids those potential problems.

> **EXAMPLE:** Matthew, an elderly widower, goes down to his bank and makes his daughter, Doris, the payable-on-death beneficiary of his checking account. Doris (and her creditors) will have no access to the money during Matthew's life, but after his death she'll be able to get the funds in the account quickly and easily.

CAUTION

Don't create a joint account just to avoid probate. If you want to leave money to someone at your death—but not give it away now—stick to a POD account. It will accomplish your goal simply and easily. Don't set up a joint account with the understanding that the other person will withdraw money only after you die. This is a common mistake, and it often creates confusion and family fights.

Adding a POD Designation to a Joint Account

POD accounts can be very useful for couples who have joint bank accounts.

Accounts With a Right of Survivorship

Most joint accounts come with what's called the "right of survivorship," meaning that when one co-owner dies, the other will automatically be the sole owner of the account. So when the first owner dies, the funds in the account belong to the survivor—without probate. If you add a POD designation, it takes effect only when the second owner dies. Then, whatever is in the account goes to the POD beneficiary you named.

> EXAMPLE: Virginia and Percy keep a joint checking account with several thousand dollars in it. They hold this account as joint tenants with right of survivorship. They decide to name their sons, who are both adults, as POD beneficiaries. After both Virginia and Percy have died, the bank will release whatever is left in the account to the sons, in equal shares.

It's important for both spouses (or other co-owners) to realize that designating a POD beneficiary for a joint account doesn't lock in the surviving spouse after one spouse dies. The survivor is free to change the beneficiary or close the account, shutting out the beneficiary who was named back when both spouses were still alive.

> EXAMPLE: Howard and Marge name Elaine, Howard's daughter from a previous marriage, as the POD payee of their joint savings account. Howard dies first, and in the years that follow relations between Marge and Elaine deteriorate. Marge decides to remove Elaine as POD beneficiary and instead name her nephew, Max. When Marge dies, Elaine doesn't inherit any of the money in the account—even though she's firmly convinced that her father intended her to.

Adding a POD beneficiary to a joint account not only avoids probate, but allows you to plan for the unlikely event that both persons die simultaneously.

> EXAMPLE: June and Horace have a joint savings account. They name their daughter, Virginia, as the payable-on-death beneficiary. When June and Horace are killed in an accident, Virginia inherits the money in the account without probate.

Accounts With No Right of Survivorship

Some kinds of joint accounts cannot be turned into payable-on-death accounts. Unless your joint account provides that when one owner dies, the other automatically becomes the sole owner, don't try to name a POD payee for the account.

Two common situations where this advice applies are:

- Your state law requires you to request the right of survivorship in writing when you open the account, and you didn't make the proper request. In that case, the account is not a joint tenancy account; it's what is known as a "tenancy in common" account, which means that you can leave your share to anyone you choose.
- You and your spouse live in a community property state and own a community property account together. Such accounts don't carry the right of survivorship; each spouse has the right to leave his or her half interest to someone else.

> (!) CAUTION
>
> **Don't use a POD designation for a joint account that doesn't have the right of survivorship.** In other words, don't try to arrange things so that a POD payee inherits just your share of a co-owned bank account at your death. It's far more reliable and less confusing to establish a separate account and name a POD payee for it.

Choosing Beneficiaries

There are few restrictions on whom you can name as a POD beneficiary. But there are some issues you should think about as you make your choices.

Extra FDIC Coverage for Beneficiaries

Payable-on-death accounts get extra coverage from the Federal Deposit Insurance Corporation.

The general rule is that the FDIC insures each person's accounts at a financial institution up to $250,000. But to calculate the amount of FDIC insurance coverage on an account with POD beneficiaries, you multiply the number of beneficiaries by $250,000.

For example, if you have an account and name your son as the POD beneficiary, your insurance coverage is $250,000, just as it would be if you had no POD beneficiary. But if you name your son and your daughter as POD beneficiaries, the account is immediately insured up to 2 × $250,000, or $500,000.

To check on FDIC coverage for your accounts, use the "Electronic Deposit Insurance Estimator" at www.fdic.gov.

Children

It's perfectly fine to name a minor—that is, a child younger than 18 years old—as a POD payee. If the account is worth more than a few thousand dollars, however, you should think about what might happen if that beneficiary were still a child at your death. You will probably want to arrange for an adult to manage the money for the child.

If you don't, and a minor child inherits money from a payable-on-death account, one of three things will happen:

- If state law allows it, the money, no matter how much, can simply be given to the beneficiary's parents (or to the beneficiary, if he or she is married). The parents hold the money for the benefit of the child.

- If the amount is relatively small—generally, a few thousand dollars, depending on state law and bank custom—the bank will probably turn it over to the child or the child's parents.
- If the amount is larger, the parents will probably have to go to court and ask to be appointed guardians of the money. (If the parents aren't alive, a guardian will probably already have been appointed and supervised by the court.)

Fortunately, court involvement, which can be expensive, intrusive, and time-consuming, can be easily avoided. You can choose someone now, and give that person authority to manage the money, without court supervision, in case the child is still younger than 18 at your death. The logical choice, usually, is one of the child's parents.

The easiest way to do this, in most states, is to name an adult to serve as "custodian" of the money. Custodians are authorized under a law called the Uniform Transfers to Minors Act (UTMA), which has been adopted by every state except South Carolina and Vermont.

All you need to do is name the custodian as the POD payee of the account and make it clear that the custodian is to act on the child's behalf. That gives the custodian the legal responsibility to manage and use the money for the benefit of the child. Then, when the child reaches adulthood, the custodian turns over what's left to the beneficiary. Most, but not all, UTMA states set 21 as the age when the custodianship ends. (The ages are listed below.)

> **EXAMPLE:** Alice wants to make her grandson, Tyler, the POD payee of a bank account. But Tyler is just nine years old. So Alice decides to name Tyler's mother, Susan, as custodian of the money in the account. On the bank's form, Alice puts, in the space for the POD payee, "Susan Irving, as custodian for Tyler Irving under the Florida Uniform Transfers to Minors Act." If Tyler is not yet 21 when his grandmother dies, Susan will be legally in charge of the money until Tyler's 21st birthday.

Age at Which an UTMA Custodianship Ends

Alabama	21	Missouri	21
Alaska	18 to 25*	Montana	21
Arizona	21	Nebraska	21
Arkansas	18 to 21*	Nevada	18 to 25*
California	18 to 25*	New Hampshire	21
Colorado	21	New Jersey	18 to 21*
Connecticut	21	New Mexico	21
Delaware	21	New York	21
District of Columbia	18 to 21*	North Carolina	18 to 21*
Florida	21	North Dakota	21
Georgia	21	Ohio	21
Hawaii	21	Oklahoma	18 to 21*
Idaho	21	Oregon	21 to 25*
Illinois	21	Pennsylvania	21 to 25*
Indiana	21	Rhode Island	21
Iowa	21	South Dakota	18
Kansas	21	Tennessee	21 to 25*
Kentucky	18	Texas	21
Louisiana	18	Utah	21
Maine	18 to 21*	Virginia	18 to 21*
Maryland	21	Washington	21 or 25
Massachusetts	21	West Virginia	21
Michigan	18 to 21*	Wisconsin	21
Minnesota	21	Wyoming	21
Mississippi	21		

* The person who sets up the custodianship can designate the age, within these limits, at which the custodianship ends and the beneficiary inherits the money outright.

> ## If You Don't Live in an UTMA State
>
> Even if you live in South Carolina or Vermont—the only states that
> haven't adopted the UTMA—you may still be able to enjoy the law's
> benefits. The law is written so that you can appoint a custodian if any
> of the following is true:
> - The custodian lives in a state that has adopted the law.
> - The minor lives in a state that has adopted the law.
> - The bank account (the "custodial property," in the terms of the
>   statute) is located in a state that has adopted the law.
>
> EXAMPLE 1: Christopher is a resident of South Carolina. His
> grandson, however, lives in California, which has adopted the
> UTMA. Christopher can appoint a custodian for his grandson
> under the California Uniform Transfers to Minors Act. As long as
> the boy is a resident of California when the transfer takes place,
> the transfer is valid under the UTMA.
>
> EXAMPLE 2: Eunice, a Vermonter, keeps an account in a New
> Hampshire bank. She can use the New Hampshire UTMA to
> appoint a custodian for her granddaughter. On the bank forms,
> she can name "Esther Stanhope, as custodian for Michelle
> Stanhope under the New Hampshire Uniform Transfers to
> Minors Act."

Multiple Beneficiaries

You may well want to name more than one person to inherit the
money in a bank account—for example, your three children or two
good friends. That's no problem; you just name all the beneficiaries
on the bank's form. Each will inherit an equal share of the money in
the account unless you specify otherwise.

CAUTION

Be careful when setting up unequal shares. In a few states—Florida, for example—you cannot change the equal-shares rule. If you're concerned about this issue, check your state's law or open a separate account for each beneficiary.

It's important to realize that you can't name an alternate payee—that is, someone to inherit the money if your first choice doesn't outlive you. In other words, if you list three payees on a bank's form, the bank won't consider your list to be a ranking in order of preference. For example, some bank forms provide three spaces for beneficiaries' names. It's not uncommon for people to assume that Beneficiary #1 will get all the money, and that if he isn't alive at your death, then #2 will inherit it, and so on. But that's not the way it works. All the beneficiaries you name will share the money in the account.

If one of the beneficiaries dies before you do, all the money will go to the surviving beneficiaries. So if you leave an account to your three children, and one of them dies before you do, the other two will inherit the funds. Depending on your family situation, this result may be fine with you—or it may not. If it's not what you want, you should name new POD payees after a beneficiary dies.

> **EXAMPLE:** Miranda names her sons, Brad and Eric, as POD beneficiaries of her bank account. Eric dies before Miranda does, leaving two children of his own. Unless Miranda changes her bank account papers to include the grandchildren as POD beneficiaries, they will not inherit their father's share. Instead, all the money in the account will belong to Brad when Miranda dies.

Also give some thought to the kind of asset you're leaving. Naming more than one POD beneficiary to inherit a bank account isn't generally a problem, because the money can easily be divided.

If you are adding a POD designation to a brokerage account, things can be more complicated. If the account owns one large asset—for example, a bond—then it will have to be sold, and the proceeds divided among all the beneficiaries. That can be done, but the sale proceeds may need to be reported to just one Social Security number, which the beneficiaries may not want. These problems can be time-consuming and costly, negating any probate-avoidance benefit.

Institutions or Businesses

It's unlikely, but your state's law may restrict your ability to name a business or an institution, such as a school, church, or another charity, as the beneficiary of a POD account. Delaware law, for example, requires the beneficiary to be "a natural person" or a nonprofit organization. (5 Del. Code Ann. § 924.) Oklahoma doesn't allow for-profit entities, such as corporations or limited liability companies, to be POD beneficiaries; beneficiaries must be individuals, trusts, or tax-exempt nonprofits. (Okla. Stat. Ann. tit. 6, § 901.)

Such a requirement can frustrate attempts to leave money as you wish. For example, under previous Georgia state law, a charitable corporation could not be the POD beneficiary of a bank account or certificates of deposit. (*Tuvim v. United Jewish Communities, Inc.,* 285 Ga. 632, 680 S.W.2d 827 (2009).) State statute, the court ruled, required POD beneficiaries to be "persons," and the definition of a person did not include corporations. Georgia amended its law in 2011 to allow charities to be beneficiaries.

Your Spouse's Rights

You may not have complete freedom to dispose of the funds in a bank account—even if it's in your name—as you wish. Your spouse or partner (if you've entered into a registered domestic partnership or civil union) may have rights, too. It depends on your state's law.

Spouses' Rights in Community Property States

If you live in a community property state, your spouse (or your registered domestic partner) probably already owns half of whatever you have in a bank account, even if the account is in your name only. If you contributed money you earned while married, that money and the interest earned on it is "community property," and your spouse is legally entitled to half.

Community Property States		Non-Community Property States
Alaska*	Nevada	All other states
Arizona	New Mexico	
California	Texas	
Idaho	Washington	
Louisiana	Wisconsin	
* Only if spouses sign a community property agreement		

CAUTION

You can't shortchange creditors or family. If you don't leave enough other assets to pay your debts and taxes or to support your spouse and minor children temporarily, a POD bank account may be subject to the claims of creditors or your family after your death. If there is any probate proceeding, your executor can demand that a POD beneficiary turn over some or all of the funds so that creditors can be paid. If you specifically pledged the account as collateral for a debt, the creditor is entitled to (and doubtless will) claim repayment directly from the funds in the account. The POD payee gets whatever, if anything, is left.

There are a few exceptions to this rule: Your money is yours to do with as you please if you and your spouse have signed a valid agreement to keep all your property separate. And your spouse does not have any right to your separate property—money you deposited before you were married, or money that you alone inherited or received as a gift—unless that money has been mixed with community property in a bank account and is impossible to separate.

If the money in your account is community property, and you want to name someone other than your spouse as the POD beneficiary for the whole account, it's a good idea to get your spouse's written consent. Otherwise, your spouse could assert a claim to half of the money in the account at your death, leaving the beneficiary you named with only half.

Spouses' Rights in Non-Community Property States

If you leave money in a POD bank account to someone other than your spouse, make sure your spouse doesn't object to your overall estate plan.

In almost all non-community property states (all states except the ones listed above), a surviving spouse who is unhappy with what the deceased spouse left him or her can claim a certain percentage of the deceased spouse's property. This is called the spouse's "elective share" or "statutory share," and in many states, it amounts to about a third of what the spouse owned. It's a rare occurrence, however, for a spouse to go to court over this, because most spouses inherit more than their statutory share.

The funds in a POD account may be subject to a spouse's claim—or they may not, depending on state law. Some states consider such accounts outside the surviving spouse's reach.

> ### Contractual Wills
>
> It's an infrequent practice these days, but some couples make legally binding agreements to leave property to each other. They sign a contract that requires them in turn to sign wills leaving all their assets (or part of them) to each other. These contracts have been ruled to take precedence over a payable-on-death designation on a bank account. In other words, the POD designation gets wiped out by the contract.
>
> > **EXAMPLE:** Scott and Terry sign a contract in which each promises to make a will leaving all their assets to the other. Later, Scott adds a payable-on-death designation to his savings account, naming his brother as the beneficiary. If Scott dies first, Terry has a legal right to the funds in the account.

If a Beneficiary Dies Before You Do

People usually choose people younger than themselves to inherit their money and property, fully expecting them to outlive their elders. But sometimes this natural course of events is disrupted. If someone you have named as a POD beneficiary dies before you do, you should change the necessary paperwork at the bank to put a new beneficiary in place.

If you named more than one payee, and one or more of them dies before you do, the funds in the account will go to the survivor(s) at your death. (See "Choosing Beneficiaries," above.)

If, however, none of the POD payees you named is alive at your death, the bank will release the funds in the account to your executor, who will be responsible for seeing that the money is distributed under the terms of your will or state law. The money will probably have to go through probate, unless your estate is small enough to qualify for special, simpler procedures. (Chapter 8 discusses these probate shortcuts.)

TIP

If you want to name alternate beneficiaries, don't rely on a POD account. Banks generally don't allow you to name an alternate POD payee—that is, someone who would inherit the money if none of your primary beneficiaries outlived you.

Your will, if you make one (and you should, for reasons like this) functions as a backup in this case, as explained below. But that doesn't avoid probate. If you want to name a backup beneficiary and be sure of avoiding probate, you'll probably want to use a living trust. (See Chapter 7.)

Depending on state law, however, the bank may be able to release the money directly to your legal heirs—the close relatives who are entitled to inherit from you if you don't leave a will. In that case, the money won't have to go through probate.

If the money goes to your executor, it will be distributed under the terms of your will, even though you most likely didn't even mention this account in your will. That's because most wills contain what is called a "residuary clause," which names a beneficiary to inherit everything that's not specifically mentioned in the will. The person you named to inherit this "residuary" property would receive this money.

> **EXAMPLE:** Mark names his brother as the POD beneficiary of his savings account. But his brother dies, and Mark, confined to a nursing home, isn't able to change the paperwork at the bank to name a new payee. Mark does, however, have a will that contains a residuary clause, naming his daughter Madeline as residuary beneficiary. When Mark dies, and the will is probated, the money in the account goes to her, along with everything else that Mark didn't specifically leave to another beneficiary.

If You Change Your Mind

Families change; relationships change. At some point you may decide that you don't want to leave money to a POD payee you've named, or a beneficiary may die before you do. You're free to change the POD arrangement, but you must meticulously follow the procedures for making changes. The law books, sadly, are full of cases brought by relatives fighting over the bank accounts of their deceased loved ones who didn't pay enough attention to these simple rules.

How to Change a POD Designation

There are two easy and foolproof ways to make a change to a POD account:

- Withdraw the money in the account, or
- Go to the bank and change the paperwork. Fill out, sign, and deliver to the bank a new account registration card that names a different beneficiary or removes the POD designation altogether.

To ensure that your wishes are followed after your death, dot the i's and cross the t's when it comes to following the bank's procedures. A change in beneficiary isn't effective unless you fulfill the bank's requirements, whatever they are. Almost all banks require something in writing—a phone call isn't good enough. And to be effective, in most places your written instructions must be received by the bank before your death.

That doesn't sound difficult, but it's not all that unusual to find problems. In one case, after a woman's death a new signature card, in a stamped envelope, was found on her desk. Relatives sued over the money. The court ruled that the change was not effective because the new signature card was ambiguous and because the bank had not received it before her death. (*Codispoti v. Mid-America Federal Savings and Loan Ass'n*, No. 85AP-451, Ohio App. (1986).)

Contradictory Will Provisions

Trying to change a POD designation in your will by leaving the account to someone else is almost certain to cause problems after your death. At best, it will spawn confusion; at worst, disagreements or even a lawsuit.

About half the states say, flat out, that a POD designation cannot be overridden or changed in a will. In these states, a will provision that purports to name a new beneficiary for a POD account will simply have no effect.

> EXAMPLE: Kimberly names her niece, Patricia, as the POD beneficiary of her bank account. After they have a falling-out, Kimberly writes her will, and in it leaves the funds in the account to her friend Charles. At Kimberly's death, Patricia is still legally entitled to collect the money.

Some other states do allow you to revoke a payable-on-death designation in your will if you specifically identify the account and the beneficiary. An attempt to wipe out several accounts with a general statement won't work. In one case, a South Dakota woman wrote in her will that "I hereby intentionally revoke any joint tenancies or trust arrangements commonly called 'Totten trusts' [another name for POD accounts] by this will." After her death, a court ruled that even this language wasn't specific enough; state law requires every POD account to be individually changed or revoked. (*In re Estate of Sneed*, 521 N.W.2d 675 (S. Dak. 1994).)

The moral: **Never rely on your will to change a payable-on-death account**. Instead, deal directly with the bank, which, after all, will be in charge of the money after your death.

Property Settlement Agreements at Divorce

A property settlement agreement, even though it's approved by a court when a couple divorces, may not revoke a payable-on-death designation.

For example, when a New York couple divorced, the property settlement agreement gave the husband "any and all bank accounts, held jointly or otherwise." Some of those accounts named the wife as payable-on-death beneficiary; when the husband died, she inherited the money. The court ruled that because the settlement agreement had not named the accounts specifically, it had not met New York's statutory requirements for the revocation of a Totten trust account. (*Eredics v. Chase Manhattan Bank, N.A.*, 760 N.Y.S.2d 737 (Ct. App. 2003).)

Similarly, when an Arizona couple divorced, their property settlement agreement gave the husband some bank CDs for which he had named the wife as the payable-on-death payee. But the husband never went to the bank and removed the wife as the POD payee. When he died, a court ruled that the ex-wife was entitled to the money, because the settlement agreement had no effect on the contract between the husband and the bank. (*Jordan v. Burgbacher,* 883 P.2d 458 (Ariz. Ct. App. 1994).)

Claiming the Money

After your death, all a POD beneficiary needs to do to claim the money is show the bank a certified copy of the death certificate and proof of his or her identity. If the account was a joint account to begin with, the bank will need to see the death certificates of all the original owners. The bank records will show that the beneficiary is entitled to whatever money is in the account.

State laws authorize banks to release the money in payable-on-death accounts when they're shown this proof of the account holder's death; they don't need probate court approval. Legally, the money automatically belongs to the beneficiaries when the original account owner dies. It's not part of the probate estate and isn't under the executor's control.

Beneficiaries may, however, encounter some delays when they go to claim the money:

- **Tax clearances.** Like other bank accounts, a payable-on-death account may be temporarily frozen at your death, if your state levies estate taxes. The bank will release the money to your beneficiaries when the state is satisfied that your estate has ample funds to pay the taxes.
- **Waiting periods.** There may be a short waiting period before the money can be claimed. Vermont, for example, doesn't allow a bank to release funds to POD beneficiaries until 90 days after the death of the account owner.

When you set up a POD account, ask the bank what the POD payee will need to do to claim the money after your death. Then make sure the payee knows what to expect.

Name a Beneficiary for Your Retirement Accounts

Choosing a Beneficiary...39

　Special Rules If You're Married or Divorced...40

　Naming Your Spouse...44

　Naming an Adult Other Than Your Spouse...46

　Naming Minor Children..47

　Naming More Than One Beneficiary...48

　Naming Your Estate..49

　Naming a Trust..49

　Naming a Charity or Another Organization...50

　Choosing Alternate Beneficiaries...51

Required Distributions From Retirement Accounts...52

　When Withdrawals Must Begin..52

　Calculating the Required Minimum Distribution...54

　Why You Don't Want to Miss a Required Distribution...55

Millions of employees and small business owners are now in charge of their own retirement plans. They are setting up and keeping an eye on their Individual Retirement Accounts (IRAs) or Keoghs, or contributing to 401(k) plans (or 403(b) plans, for employees of nonprofit organizations or public schools) under programs set up by their employers. Americans had $18 trillion socked away for retirement at the end of 2011, according to the Federal Reserve System Board of Governors.

These accounts offer tax breaks now and retirement income later. And even after your death, they can give more benefits for your family because they avoid probate, too. Any money left in one of these accounts at your death goes to the beneficiaries you chose—without going through probate.

When a beneficiary withdraws the money from a 401(k) plan or traditional IRA after your death, the tax deferral ends; the money is treated as taxable income of the beneficiary. This is unlike other inherited assets, which are not subject to income tax. Money withdrawn from a Roth IRA, however, generally is not taxed.

The IRS publishes thick books containing nothing but retirement plan rules. These regulations are often next to impossible to figure out, and of course they can change at any time. This chapter focuses on the relatively simple task of choosing a beneficiary to inherit the money without probate. It also touches on some important IRS rules about required withdrawals from the two most common types of retirement plans, IRAs and 401(k) plans.

The Tax Advantages of Retirement Plans

Traditional IRAs and 401(k) Plans. First, the money you deposit each year (up to the legal limit, which depends on the type of retirement plan) is tax deductible. That means at income tax time, you can reduce your taxable income by the amount of your contribution.

Second, the income and profits that come from investing the money you save generally aren't taxed now, either. All of it can be reinvested and start earning income itself.

Of course, nothing good lasts forever. Eventually, you must start making withdrawals, and when you do, the money you take out will be subject to income tax (unless some of your contributions were not tax deductible). By then, however, presumably you'll be retired and in a lower tax bracket. (Internal Rev. Code §§ 72, 219.)

Roth IRAs. The Roth IRA is a whole different animal. Contributions are not tax deductible. Income accumulates tax free, however, as long as the contributions stay in the account at least five years. Most important, qualified withdrawals are not taxed. There are no mandatory lifetime withdrawals.

Choosing a Beneficiary

When you create an IRA or enroll in a 401(k) plan, the forms you fill out will ask you to name a beneficiary. You will probably also be given the opportunity to name an alternate (sometimes called "secondary" or "contingent") beneficiary, who will inherit the money if your first choice dies before you do or at the same time.

Always fill out the beneficiary form! Even if, for example, you're sure that your spouse would inherit the funds in the account, name your spouse as beneficiary. If you don't, the funds will have to go through probate on the way to your spouse—a detour that wastes time and money.

Choosing who will inherit the funds in your retirement account is, obviously, a very important decision. If you're single, you're free to choose whomever you want as the beneficiary. If you're married, however, the law may restrict your choices significantly.

Naming a Retirement Account Beneficiary at a Glance	
Pros	**Cons**
• Easy and free to set up. • You can change your mind and name a different beneficiary at any time (subject to certain rights of your spouse). • It's easy for the beneficiary to claim the money after your death.	• Your retirement plan may not allow you to name an alternate beneficiary. • Federal law requires mandatory withdrawals from traditional IRAs and from 401(k) accounts.

Special Rules If You're Married or Divorced

Most married people choose their spouses to inherit the money in retirement accounts. It's often a good choice for financial reasons as well as personal ones, as discussed below.

If you want to name a different beneficiary, you may run into complications from several state and federal laws intended to make sure your spouse isn't left out in the cold if you die first. The effect of these laws depends on the kind of retirement account you have and where you live.

CAUTION

Get your spouse's consent in writing. No matter what kind of retirement account you have, it's always a good idea—and may be required by law, as discussed below—to get your spouse's written consent before naming someone else as beneficiary.

Don't Rely on Your Divorce Decree

If your former spouse's name is still on a beneficiary designation form for any kind of retirement benefit, change it. Do it even if you think your divorce settlement agreement makes it clear that your ex is no longer entitled to anything.

If you don't, the former spouse could end up inheriting the benefit. That's what happened to a Texas couple. The wife, a retired teacher, had named her husband as the beneficiary of an annuity she received from the teachers' retirement system. Under state law, she couldn't name a different beneficiary without the written consent of her spouse or a court order.

When she and her husband divorced, the divorce decree stated that the husband had no more rights to his wife's retirement benefits—but didn't mention the annuity specifically. And she never got her ex-husband's consent to name a new beneficiary. As a result, when the woman died, her ex-husband was legally entitled to the annuity benefits. (*Holmes v. Kent*, 221 S.W.3d 622 (Tex. 2007).)

401(k) Plans

A special rule applies to 401(k) plans (and other "qualified plans"): Your spouse is entitled to inherit all the money in the account *unless* he or she signs a written waiver, consenting to your choice of another beneficiary. It's not enough just to name someone else on the beneficiary form that your employer gives you.

Especially if your spouse will be well provided for from other sources, the two of you may decide it makes sense to leave the money to someone else. If your spouse agrees to sign the waiver, which should be provided by the firm that administers the 401(k) plan, a plan representative or a notary public must act as a witness. A prenuptial agreement can't take the place of a waiver; the law says the *spouse* (not soon-to-be-spouse) must sign. A spouse who does sign a waiver can withdraw that consent if the other spouse later names a different beneficiary, unless the signing spouse expressly gave up that right. (IRC § 417(a)(2).)

Divorce. If you name your spouse as beneficiary of a 401(k) plan, pension plan, or employer-provided life insurance policy, and later divorce, a number of states have laws that automatically revoke your ex-spouse's right to inherit. These laws are no longer valid, under a ruling made by the U.S. Supreme Court. (*Egelhoff v. Egelhoff,* 532 U.S. 141 (2001).)

The Court's decision was based on the fact that 401(k) and similar plans, including severance plans and employee savings accounts, are governed by a federal law, the Employee Retirement Income Security Act (ERISA). That law, the Court ruled, requires the plan administrator to simply pay the proceeds to the beneficiary named by the plan participant—not to figure out who should get them under a particular state's law. (In 2009, the Court ruled the same way in a similar case, *Kennedy v. Plan Administrator for DuPont Savings & Investment Plan,* 555 U.S. 285.)

Individual Retirement Accounts

If you don't live in a community property state (listed below), you are free to name whomever you wish as your IRA beneficiary, even if you're married.

If, however, you live in a community property state, read on. Chances are your spouse or registered domestic partner owns half of what you have socked away in a retirement account. If any of the money you contributed was earned while you were married, that money remains "community property," and your spouse owns half.

Community Property States	
Alaska*	Nevada
Arizona	New Mexico
California	Texas
Idaho	Washington
Louisiana	Wisconsin
* Only if spouses sign a community property agreement	

There are a few exceptions to this rule: Your spouse does not have any right to money you contributed before you were married or money that you alone inherited or were given. And the money you earned is yours to do with as you please if you and your spouse signed a valid agreement to keep all your property separate.

If the money in your retirement account is community property, and you want to name someone other than your spouse as the beneficiary, get your spouse's consent in writing. Some retirement plans, in fact, won't let you name someone else without this consent. If your spouse doesn't consent, the beneficiary you name will be entitled to only half of what's in the retirement account at your death.

State law may set out the rules about your spouse's consent. For example, in California, the spouse's consent must be in writing. The spouse can revoke the consent, again in writing, anytime before your death—in a will, for example. To be effective, the revocation must be delivered to you in a manner set out by the statute. (Cal. Prob. Code § 2031.)

Naming Your Spouse

If, like the great majority of married people, you want to name your husband or wife to inherit your retirement savings, you're making a good choice. A surviving spouse who is the sole beneficiary has more flexibility about what to do with the money than do other beneficiaries. Unlike other beneficiaries, who must start to withdraw the money in the year after your death (though not necessarily all at once, as discussed below), a surviving spouse, in some cases, can keep *all* the money tax deferred at least for a while. (This isn't a concern with the Roth IRA, because withdrawals generally aren't taxed.)

A surviving spouse's options are basically the same whether the account owner dies before or after reaching the age at which required minimum withdrawals (discussed below) must begin. There is, however, one significant exception: If the minimum withdrawals have become necessary, then the surviving spouse must make the withdrawal for the year of death. After that, he or she can exercise one of the following choices.

Roll Over the Account

A spouse who is the sole beneficiary can "roll over" the money in the retirement account (IRA or qualified plan such as a 401(k)) to his or her own IRA. To do that, the spouse needs to contact the retirement account administrator and complete some paperwork.

Once the account has been rolled over, everything is just as if the surviving spouse were the original owner. The surviving spouse can name a beneficiary to inherit the funds at his or her death. Required minimum distributions will begin at age 70½, and the amounts will be based on his or her life expectancy as set out in IRS tables. (Or, if the spouse remarries, required withdrawals will be based on the joint life expectancy of the survivor and the new spouse.)

The surviving spouse doesn't have to pay income tax on money in the account until it is withdrawn. Meanwhile, the funds can keep earning tax-deferred income.

A rollover can happen at any time—the survivor could do it years after the spouse's death. There's rarely a reason to wait. It might make sense, however, if the survivor is under age 59½ and wants to withdraw money from the account. Beneficiaries are not subject to the usual 10% "early distribution" (before age 59½) penalty, but they lose that special exemption if they roll over the account.

> **EXAMPLE:** Annie is 45, with two children still at home, when her husband dies and she inherits the money in his 401(k) plan account. She may need to withdraw money from the account in the next few years.
>
> If she rolled over the money into her own retirement account, and then withdrew some of it before age 59½, she would have to pay the 10% early withdrawal penalty. So instead, she leaves the money in her late husband's account. It will continue to earn income that won't be taxed until she withdraws it, and she can make withdrawals without penalty.

Leave the Account in the Deceased Spouse's Name

A spouse who is the sole beneficiary can leave the retirement account in the deceased spouse's name. The survivor must begin taking required distributions by the later of:

- December 31 of the year after the deceased spouse's death, or
- the year the deceased spouse would have turned 70½.

The survivor can name a beneficiary, but the amount of the minimum required distributions is determined by the surviving spouse's life expectancy, as found in the IRS single life expectancy table, not the uniform table that assumes a beneficiary who is ten years younger.

SEE AN EXPERT
Your surviving spouse may need professional advice. When your beneficiary eventually inherits the money in your retirement account—which, of course, might be many years down the line—he or she may want to get advice from a knowledgeable tax, investment, or pension specialist. IRS rules change, as do investment strategies, and your beneficiary will want to know the pros and cons of all options available under the current law.

Naming an Adult Other Than Your Spouse

Subject to your spouse's rights (this very important restriction is discussed above), you can name whomever you want to inherit your qualified plan or IRA.

If you name two or more persons as beneficiaries, they will get equal shares unless you specify otherwise in the documents that set up the account.

Nonspouse beneficiaries who inherit an IRA or 401(k) account can never roll the account over into their own accounts; only spouses can do that. But other beneficiaries do have options that can let them keep the money in the account growing tax deferred.

Create an "Inherited IRA"

A nonspouse beneficiary can create a special "inherited IRA" for the money in an IRA or qualified plan. This way, the funds can continue to grow tax deferred in the new IRA. Required minimum withdrawals are based on the beneficiary's statistical life expectancy.

There are important rules to follow to roll an inherited 401(k) plan into an IRA, and a beneficiary who doesn't follow them will end up paying tax after all. Here are the key requirements:

- Nonspouse beneficiaries cannot transfer 401(k) funds into existing IRAs; they must instead set up new "inherited IRAs."
- The trustee of a 401(k) plan must transfer the money directly to the new IRA (a "trustee-to-trustee transfer"). If the

beneficiary takes the money, then turns around and puts it into an IRA, income tax will be due on the amount.

Beneficiaries' Required Withdrawals

Someone who inherits a retirement account must make required minimum withdrawals, even before reaching retirement age.

If you die before you are required to take minimum distributions from your account. IRS rules allow the beneficiary you named (your spouse or someone else) to withdraw the money in your account over his or her own life expectancy.

If the beneficiary doesn't need all the money right away, spreading out the withdrawals offers several advantages. Obviously, it lets the beneficiary postpone paying the income tax that is due when money is withdrawn. And if the money were taken in a lump sum over just a few years, it might bump the recipient into a higher tax bracket.

If you die after required minimum distributions have begun. In the year of death, the beneficiary you named must withdraw as much as you would have been required to. After that, minimum distributions are based on the life expectancy of your beneficiary. That person looks up his or her life expectancy (from an IRS table) and then subtracts one every year.

For a Roth IRA, which has no mandatory lifetime withdrawals, the options for beneficiaries remain the same as if the IRA were a conventional one and the death had occurred before required minimum withdrawals had begun.

Naming Minor Children

You can name a minor—that is, a child younger than 18 years old— as the beneficiary of your retirement account. In fact, children are common beneficiaries; single parents may name their own children, and grandparents may wish to leave some money directly to grandchildren. Or you may have a favorite young relative or friend you'd like to help out. And even if you don't name a child as your primary beneficiary, you may well want to name one as an alternate.

There is, however, a potential problem. If that beneficiary is still a minor at your death, you will want to arrange for an adult to manage the money.

If you don't make some arrangements, and a child inherits more than a few thousand dollars, the child's parents, if they're alive, will probably have to go to court and ask to be appointed guardians of the money. If neither parent is alive, the child's court-appointed and court-supervised guardian will handle the child's money.

Fortunately, this layer of court involvement, which can be expensive, intrusive, and time-consuming, can be easily avoided. You can choose someone now and give that person authority to manage the money without court supervision, in case the beneficiary inherits the money while still a minor. The logical choice, usually, is one of the child's parents.

The easiest way to do this, if your state law allows it, is to name an adult to serve as "custodian" of the money. Custodians are authorized under a law called the Uniform Transfers to Minors Act (UTMA), which has been adopted by all but a few states. The UTMA is explained in detail in Chapter 1.

Naming More Than One Beneficiary

It's generally a bad idea to name more than one beneficiary. There are a couple of reasons.

First, if you name your spouse and someone else as cobeneficiaries, your spouse loses some special benefits and flexibility (see above).

Second, it complicates things. If you die before age 70½, then multiple beneficiaries can split your account, and each can use his or her own life expectancy to determine the minimum amount they must withdraw each year. But if your beneficiaries inherit after you had reached age 70½ and had to begin making minimum withdrawals (discussed below), the total amount that must be withdrawn each year is based on the statistical life expectancy of the oldest beneficiary. If some beneficiaries are much older than others, the younger ones will have to withdraw money (and pay tax on it) more quickly than they may wish to.

One possible solution, if you want several beneficiaries to share the money: Split the account yourself, now, and name just one beneficiary for each smaller account.

Naming Your Estate

You can name your own estate as the beneficiary of a retirement plan—but doing so ensures that the money in the account will have to go through probate before being distributed. And if you die before age 70½, all the money will have to be withdrawn in five years. If you die after age 70½, whoever inherits the account will have to continue making withdrawals as fast as you would have. So the smart course is simple: Don't do it.

Naming a Trust

If you've set up a living trust to avoid probate (see Chapter 7), good for you—but you probably should not name your trust as the beneficiary of your retirement accounts. Some companies have stopped allowing their employees to name trusts as beneficiaries of their retirement plans.

First of all, you don't need a living trust to avoid probate for the money in a retirement account. If you name a beneficiary (as long as you don't name your estate), the money won't go through probate. You might use a trust to provide management for the funds if you expect the beneficiaries to be under age 18 when they inherit, but this is a fairly unusual situation. The trust must meet certain IRS regulations.

A potential drawback to naming a trust is that the trust beneficiary won't be able to name new beneficiaries. For example, if you create a trust for your spouse and name the trust as the beneficiary of your retirement plan money, your spouse will be provided for. But she won't be able to roll over the account into her own retirement account and name her own beneficiaries, perhaps your children. Those children, in turn, could have kept the money tax deferred, taking out only small minimum required distributions based on their long life expectancies.

If you do name a revocable living trust as the beneficiary of your retirement account, required minimum distributions after your death will be based on the life expectancy of the oldest trust beneficiary (if the beneficiary is a person, not an institution). Because an older beneficiary has a shorter life expectancy, minimum payouts are larger—shortening the time the money stays in the tax-deferred account. A younger beneficiary could lose 25 years of tax savings. If there is more than one beneficiary, they must all receive equal distributions.

Naming a Charity or Another Organization

You can name a charity or institution as the beneficiary of your retirement account. While you're alive, minimum required distributions are based on the IRS Uniform table, which assumes that you have a beneficiary ten years younger than you are.

After your death, the charity must take out the money within five years (if you die before you reach age 70½) or take distributions based on your life expectancy (if you die after age 70½). Minimum distributions usually aren't a problem for charities, which are happy to cash out the accounts they inherit. But if you name a person and a charity as cobeneficiaries, after your death, the IRS treats the situation as if you had not named a beneficiary at all, meaning distributions will be accelerated for the individual beneficiary as well as the charity.

Choosing Alternate Beneficiaries

When you name your primary beneficiary, you'll probably be able to name an alternate—someone to inherit the money if your first choice doesn't survive you. Alternates are also called contingent or secondary beneficiaries. Most people who are married with children name their spouses as the primary beneficiaries, and their children as the alternates.

> EXAMPLE: Frances names (on the form she gets from the account administrator) her husband Sean as the primary beneficiary of her IRA. She doesn't name a secondary (alternate) beneficiary. Years later, Sean, now in his 80s, dies, and Frances dies soon after—without updating the beneficiary paperwork.
>
> Because there is no designated beneficiary, the money becomes part of Frances's estate. Under the terms of her will, the money will pass to her son Colin, who must withdraw it all within five years. Had Colin been named as the alternate beneficiary, he could have withdrawn the money over his own life expectancy—more than 40 years.

Naming an alternate beneficiary also gives your family more flexibility after your death. It's easy for a beneficiary to "disclaim" his or her inheritance—that is, to turn it down in favor of the alternate beneficiary. Why would someone turn down money? An older spouse, for example, simply might not need it. By letting it go to the children instead, withdrawals could be spread out over a longer period.

> EXAMPLE: Harvey names his wife, Marlene, as the primary beneficiary of his IRA and his son, Matthew, as the secondary beneficiary. When Harvey dies, Marlene is in her 70s and doesn't need the money in the IRA. She would rather it go to Matthew, so he could stretch distributions over his much longer

life expectancy and let the money in the account continue to grow. So she disclaims her interest in the money, letting it pass directly to Matthew.

SEE AN EXPERT

Disclaimers can get tricky. To make a disclaimer successfully, you must pay careful attention to IRS rules and deadlines. Get expert advice.

Required Distributions From Retirement Accounts

If you save and invest wisely, you can leave a substantial amount in an individual retirement account—but for most accounts, there are limits. The IRS wants to keep these accounts restricted to their original purpose of providing a decent income during your retirement. You (or your beneficiaries) will be in for severe financial penalties if you violate the rules.

Roth IRAs. There are no required distributions from Roth IRAs. As a result, a Roth IRA could contain a much larger amount at your death than a comparable traditional IRA or 401(k)—and pass that larger amount on without probate.

When Withdrawals Must Begin

The ideal scenario, in the eyes of the IRS, would be to have you exhaust the money in your retirement account at precisely the moment you breathe your last. That's why the IRS makes you start withdrawing money in your 70s, and why the amount of these required minimum distributions is tied to your statistical life expectancy.

Traditional IRAs. Distributions become mandatory the year you turn age 70½. (The rules already sound confusing, don't they? It's not too bad—take a deep breath and read on.) The IRS bases

Retirement Account Withdrawal Rules: A Summary

Your Age	Withdrawal Rules
Younger than 59½ "Premature" withdrawals	**Traditional IRAs:** Withdrawals are subject to a 10% penalty, unless you become disabled and cannot work, you die, you use the money to buy your first house, or you set up a plan to make regular, equal withdrawals over your life. You cannot borrow from an IRA.
	Roth IRAs: Withdrawals of contributions are always tax free. Qualified withdrawals of earnings are penalty and tax free if you've had the account for at least five years and you are disabled or are using the money to buy your first house (up to $10,000).
	401(k) plans: You can borrow from your 401(k), but cannot withdraw money from it except for an IRS-recognized hardship, such as to pay medical bills, prevent eviction or foreclosure, pay college tuition, or make a down payment on your primary residence. And you still must pay the 10% penalty on early withdrawals. There is one important exception: If you're 55 or older and actually retired, you may make penalty-free withdrawals.
59½ to 70½ "Ordinary" withdrawals	Withdrawals are optional.
	Traditional IRAs: The amount is included in your gross income for income tax purposes.
	Roth IRAs: Withdrawals of contributions and of qualified earnings are not taxed.
70½ or older "Required" distributions	**Traditional IRAs and 401(k)s:** Withdrawals are required. The minimum amount is determined by your age.
	Roth IRAs: Withdrawals are optional.

everything on calendar years. You must make one whole year's withdrawal for the calendar year in which you turn 70½. This first year, however, you get a bit of extra time before you actually have to take out the money: You have until April 1 of the following year to make the withdrawal. After that, the deadline is always December 31.

> **EXAMPLE:** Robert turns 70½ on November 30, 2010. He must make a full year's required minimum distribution for 2010, but he has until April 1, 2011, to do it. He must take 2011's required minimum distribution by December 31, 2011.

401(k) Accounts. You don't have to withdraw money from your 401(k) account until you turn 70½ or you actually retire, whichever is later. (There's one exception: If you're self-employed, you must begin withdrawals at 70½.) If you retire after you are 70½, then April 1 of the following year is the date by which you must make your first required distribution.

Calculating the Required Minimum Distribution

The minimum amount you must withdraw is based on your life expectancy and that of a beneficiary. The IRS provides a table on which you can look up this "joint life expectancy"; then you simply divide the amount in your account by this number and take out the result.

> **EXAMPLE:** Valerie is 75; the IRS Uniform Distribution Period Table gives her a figure of 13.4 years. The balance in her IRA at the end of the previous calendar year was $50,000, so this year she must withdraw $2,294.

Whether or not you actually name a beneficiary, the IRS table assumes that your beneficiary is ten years younger than you are. You don't need to consider the beneficiary's actual age unless the beneficiary is your spouse and is in fact more than ten years younger than you. In that case, you can reduce the amount you must withdraw by using a different IRS table that factors in your spouse's actual age.

> **EXAMPLE 1:** Jason turns 70½ on February 23. That means by April 1 of the next calendar year, he must have made a year's worth of withdrawals from his IRA account. His wife, Molly, the beneficiary of the IRA, is four years younger than he is.
>
> To calculate the minimum amount he must withdraw, Jason will have to look up his age in the IRS Uniform Distribution Table. The table assumes that Molly is ten years younger than Jason, which works to their benefit—the minimum amounts Jason must withdraw each year will be smaller than if Molly's actual life expectancy were used.

> **EXAMPLE 2:** Mark names his wife Rita, who is 12 years his junior, as his IRA beneficiary. To calculate his required minimum distribution, he uses the IRS table that calculates his and Rita's joint life expectancy based on their actual ages.

Why You Don't Want to Miss a Required Distribution

If you don't make the legally required withdrawal, you will forfeit half of the amount you should have withdrawn but didn't. That's right: There's a full 50% tax on the money you shouldn't have left in the account.

> **EXAMPLE:** When Mae is required to begin taking money from her IRA, she dutifully makes a withdrawal—but mistakenly takes out $1,000 less than she should. The next year, when she files her income tax return, she must pay $500 in extra tax (and file an extra form).

RESOURCE

More information. *IRAs, 401(k)s & Other Retirement Plans: Taking Your Money Out,* by Twila Slesnick and John C. Suttle (Nolo), contains a thorough discussion of the rules that govern withdrawals from the most common kinds of retirement plans.

The website www.rothira.com contains news, articles, calculators, links, and much more, all dealing with various aspects of the Roth IRA.

Name a Beneficiary for Your Stocks and Bonds

Transfer-on-Death Registration 58

    Who Can Use the Law 59

    How It Works 61

    Joint Accounts 62

    Your Spouse's Rights 63

    Naming Children as Beneficiaries 64

    Naming More Than One TOD Beneficiary 65

    If a Beneficiary Dies Before You Do 66

    If You Change Your Mind 67

    When Not to Use TOD Registration 67

    Claiming the Securities 67

Registration of Government Bonds and Notes 67

Several factors have combined to produce a tremendous flood of money into the stock market in the last few decades. Many working people, suddenly in charge of their own retirement investments, began to store up money in IRAs and 401(k) plans, and invested the funds in the market. Investing in stocks or bonds became simpler and less risky with the advent of widely advertised mutual funds, with their diversified holdings. And discount brokers made buying and selling individual stocks less costly.

As a result, many ordinary Americans now have sizable amounts tied up in corporate and government securities instead of plain old bank accounts, savings bonds, or certificates of deposit. To their credit, state lawmakers have responded to this important shift with what passes for lightning speed in the legislative world. In fewer than ten years, almost every state has authorized a simple way for people to leave securities to their loved ones without probate.

Transfer-on-Death Registration

Every state except Louisiana and Texas has adopted a law that lets you name someone to inherit your stocks, bonds, or brokerage accounts without probate. It works very much like a payable-on-death bank account (explained in Chapter 1). When you register your ownership, either with the stockbroker or the company itself, you make a request to take ownership in what's called "beneficiary form." When the papers that show your ownership are issued, they will also show the name of your beneficiary.

After you have registered ownership this way, the beneficiary has no rights to the stock as long as you are alive. You are free to sell it, give it away, name a different beneficiary, or close the account. But on your death, the beneficiary can claim the securities without probate, simply by providing proof of death and some identification to the broker or transfer agent. (A transfer agent is a business that is authorized by a corporation to transfer ownership of its stock from one person to another.)

The law that allows transfer-on-death registration is called the Uniform Transfer-on-Death Securities Registration Act.

Beneficiary Registration at a Glance	
Pros	**Cons**
• Easy to create. • Designating a beneficiary costs nothing (though some brokers may charge a fee to change beneficiaries). • It's easy for the beneficiary to claim the securities after the original owner dies.	• Your broker might not allow you to name an alternate beneficiary.

Who Can Use the Law

If you live in any state but Louisiana or Texas, you can register any stocks or mutual fund shares in beneficiary form. Even if you live in one of these two states, however, you may be able to register your stocks in a transfer-on-death form. That's because the way the uniform law is written, if either the stock owner or the stock issuer has any connection to a state that has passed the law, transfer-on-death registration is available.

You can register ownership of a stock or a mutual fund account in beneficiary form if *any* of the following is true:

- You live in a state that has adopted the law.
- The stockbroker's principal office is located in a state that has adopted the law.
- The issuer of the stock or the stockbroker ("registering entity") is incorporated in a state that has adopted the law.

- The transfer agent's office is located in a state that has adopted the law.
- The office making the registration is in a state that has adopted the law.

EXAMPLE 1: Sophia is a resident of Florida, which has adopted the Transfer-on-Death Security Registration Act. She can register any stock or brokerage account she owns in beneficiary form, regardless of where the company that issues or registers the stock is located.

EXAMPLE 2: Ben lives in Texas, which has not passed the Act. But he maintains a brokerage account with Cascade Mutual Fund, which has its main office in the state of Washington, which has adopted the Act. He can name a transfer-on-death beneficiary and avoid probate of the account.

EXAMPLE 3: Ben also owns some stock of the Olde Cudahy Cheese Works, Inc., a company incorporated in Wisconsin. Because Wisconsin has adopted the Act, Ben can register ownership of his shares in beneficiary form.

> **TIP**
> **Your broker may not cooperate.** Although a good many stockbrokers, corporations, and transfer agents offer transfer-on-death registration, the law does not require them to; it merely gives them the option of doing so. If your state passed the uniform law recently, you may even have to educate your broker about it—or, if that fails, move your account.

How It Works

It's a simple process to register ownership of your stocks in beneficiary (also called transfer-on-death, or TOD) form. The exact procedure, however, depends on whether you hold your stocks in a brokerage account or you actually have stock certificates sent to you.

If you have a brokerage account (or more than one, as many people do), you should contact the broker for instructions. Most likely, the broker will send you a form on which you'll name one or more beneficiaries to inherit the stocks in your account at your death. From then on, the account will be listed in your name, with the beneficiary's name after it, like this:

"Evelyn M. Meyers, TOD Charles Meyers."

If you have the actual stock certificates or bonds in your possession —most people don't—you must get new certificates issued, showing that you now own the stock in beneficiary form. Ask your broker for help. If the broker is unable or unwilling to help, write to the transfer agent for the stock. You can get the address from your broker or the investor relations office of the corporation. The transfer agent will explain what to do. You'll probably have to send in the certificates and a form called a stock or bond power, which you must fill out and sign (some stock certificates have the power printed on the back) and a letter explaining what you want to do.

Gift and Estate Tax Concerns

You keep complete control over the securities for which you name a transfer-on-death beneficiary, so you're not, in legal terms, making a gift when you register stocks in beneficiary form. That means you don't have to worry about federal gift tax.

Naming a beneficiary has no effect on federal estate taxes, either. At your death, the value of the stocks is included in your estate for federal estate tax purposes, just as it would have been had you not named a transfer-on-death beneficiary.

Joint Accounts

If you own stock or mutual fund shares together with another person—your wife or husband, for example—you can still name a transfer-on-death beneficiary. But there's an important restriction: You and the co-owner must have "rights of survivorship" in the account. That means that when the first owner dies, the survivor automatically takes full ownership. That's how most joint accounts are set up. The transfer-on-death beneficiary inherits the stock only after both original owners have died.

Incidentally, this also takes care of a common concern of many couples: what will happen if they die simultaneously.

> **EXAMPLE:** Helen and Chase own a mutual fund account together. On the account documents, their names are listed this way: "Helen Whittaker, Chase Whittaker JT TEN WROS." That means that they own the account as joint tenants with the right of survivorship—the legal way of saying that they share ownership 50-50, and when Helen or Chase dies, the survivor will automatically own the entire account.
>
> When Helen and Chase decide to add their grown children, Amanda and Jeffrey, as transfer-on-death beneficiaries, the ownership documents are changed to include this odd-looking string of words: "Helen Whittaker, Chase Whittaker JT TEN WROS, TOD Amanda S. Whittaker and Jeffrey R. Whittaker." The TOD stands for "transfer on death."

After one joint owner dies, the other is free to change the beneficiary designation. So naming a TOD beneficiary while both joint owners are alive doesn't guarantee that that beneficiary will ultimately inherit the securities.

EXAMPLE: Jane and Henry name Henry's son from a previous marriage as the TOD beneficiary of a jointly held stock account. After Henry dies, Jane is the sole owner, and decides to change the beneficiary to someone else. Henry's son won't inherit any of the stocks.

TIP
You can lock in a beneficiary. If you're concerned that after your death, the surviving co-owner of a joint account might change the beneficiary in a way you wouldn't approve of, create a separate account in your name only, and name the beneficiary. (But if you're married, you should still get your spouse's consent; this is discussed next.)

Your Spouse's Rights

You may not have complete freedom to dispose of your securities—even if they're registered in your name—as you wish. Your spouse may have rights, too. The extent of those rights depends on your state's law.

Community Property States		Non-Community Property States
Alaska*	Nevada	All other states
Arizona	New Mexico	
California	Texas	
Idaho	Washington	
Louisiana	Wisconsin	
* Only if spouses sign a community property agreement		

Spouses' Rights in Community Property States

If you live in a community property state, your spouse (or registered domestic partner) may well own half of whatever securities you own, even if you hold them in your name only. If you bought securities with money you earned while married, they are "community property," and your spouse legally owns a half share unless you and your spouse signed a valid agreement to keep all your property separate.

If you have a securities account registered in your name only, and you want to name someone other than your spouse as the TOD beneficiary for it, it's a good idea to get your spouse's written consent. Otherwise, if your spouse objects, he or she could assert a claim to half of the money in the account at your death, leaving the beneficiary you named with only half.

Spouses' Rights in Non-Community Property States

If you leave stocks to someone other than your spouse, make sure your spouse doesn't object to your overall estate plan.

In most non-community property states, surviving spouses who are unhappy with what the deceased spouse left them can claim a certain percentage of the deceased spouse's property. This is called the spouse's "statutory share," and in many states it amounts to about a third of what the spouse owned. It's rare, however, for a spouse to go to court over this, because most spouses inherit more than their statutory share.

The funds in a TOD account may be subject to a spouse's claim—or they may not, depending on state law. Some states consider such accounts outside the surviving spouse's reach.

Naming Children as Beneficiaries

You can name a minor—that is, a child younger than 18 years old—as a transfer-on-death beneficiary, but doing so raises some legal issues you should deal with. Every state's law forbids children younger than 18 from controlling substantial amounts of property themselves, without an adult's supervision. The dollar limit varies from state to state, but it's fair to say that anything worth more than a few thousand dollars necessitates an adult manager for the money.

Fortunately, it's not difficult to take care of this potential complication. You can choose someone now to manage the money if the beneficiary you've chosen inherits the money while still a minor. In most states, you can appoint this person on the registration document by naming him or her as a "custodian" of the property.

> **EXAMPLE:** Tess wants to leave stock to her ten-year-old nephew, Sam, but wants his mother to manage it in case Sam inherits it while he is still a child. On the ownership registration document, she names the TOD beneficiary as "Amelia Tompkins, as custodian for Samuel Tompkins under the Indiana Uniform Transfers to Minors Act."

For more detailed information about custodianship under the Uniform Transfers to Minors Act, see Chapter 1.

Naming More Than One TOD Beneficiary

If you want to name more than one beneficiary, just name all the beneficiaries on the form. Each will inherit an equal share of the stocks unless you specify otherwise. You can, however, leave the beneficiaries unequal shares if the stockbroker or transfer agent's policy allows it. (If you do, double-check your percentages and make sure they add up to 100%, or the fractions to 1. It's easier than you might think to make a mistake.)

> **EXAMPLE:** Martha lists her four children as the TOD beneficiaries of her mutual fund shares. She decides to leave one of her children, who has a disabled child and could use

more financial help, a larger share than the rest. She registers ownership of the mutual fund shares this way: "Martha Levenson, TOD Frank Levenson 20%, Elizabeth Levenson 20%, Emily Levenson-Thompson 20%, David Levenson 40%."

If a Beneficiary Dies Before You Do

You can name an alternate beneficiary, if your broker's policies allow it, when you register securities in transfer-on-death form. If you do, and the primary TOD beneficiary dies before you do, the alternate will inherit.

> **EXAMPLE:** Francis names his wife as the TOD beneficiary of his mutual fund account and his daughter Marie as contingent (alternate) beneficiary. His wife dies, and Francis doesn't get around to changing the paperwork to name a new beneficiary. When Francis dies, the account goes to Marie.

If you don't name an alternate, the stock will probably pass under your will's "residuary clause," which names a beneficiary to inherit everything that's not specifically mentioned in the will. Your "residuary beneficiary" would inherit the securities.

If you name more than one beneficiary, and one or more of them dies before you do, the securities will go to the survivor(s) at your death.

> **EXAMPLE:** Cheryl's children, Zachary and Grace, are the TOD beneficiaries of her brokerage account. Zachary dies before Cheryl does, leaving three children of his own. If Cheryl wants these grandchildren to inherit their father's share, she must change her account registration papers to include them as TOD beneficiaries. Otherwise, at her death, the account will belong solely to Grace.

If You Change Your Mind

You are always free to change the TOD beneficiary of your securities. The beneficiary's consent—or knowledge—is not required. To make a change, contact the broker or transfer agent. You must redo the ownership document itself for the change to take effect.

When Not to Use TOD Registration

As useful as it can be, TOD registration is not always a good idea. In general, stay away from it if you want to name multiple beneficiaries and the securities aren't easily divisible. Trying to divide a single bond, for example, among three children can get very worky.

Claiming the Securities

After your death, all the beneficiary needs to do to claim the stocks is show the transfer agent or broker a certified copy of the death certificate and proof of his or her identity. If the account was a joint account to begin with and wasn't ever changed to the name of the survivor, the beneficiary will need the death certificates of all the original owners. The broker's or transfer agent's records themselves will show that the beneficiary is entitled to the securities.

Once the broker has the necessary documents, the securities or the account can be reregistered in the new owner's name. No probate court approval is required. Legally, the securities automatically belong to the beneficiaries when the original owner dies.

Registration of Government Bonds and Notes

You can also name someone to inherit certain kinds of government securities, including Treasury bills and notes and savings bonds.

To do this, register ownership of the securities in "beneficiary" form. You simply register ownership in your name, followed by the words "payable on death to" and the name of your beneficiary. The beneficiary must be a person, not an organization. (31 C.F.R. Parts 315.6 and 353.6.) If the beneficiary is a minor, you must specify that—for example, by writing "payable on death to Jasmine Martin, a minor." After your death, ownership will be transferred to the person you named.

As with corporate securities, you'll have complete control over these assets. You don't need the beneficiary's consent to sell or give away the securities, and you can name a different beneficiary at any time by filling out new ownership documents.

One significant limitation on adding a payable-on-death beneficiary is that there may be only one primary owner and one beneficiary. You can't name a payable-on-death beneficiary if the securities are co-owned by two or more people—you and your spouse, for example. In that situation, the best you can do is to create a right of survivorship, so that the surviving co-owner inherits the securities when the first co-owner dies. Then, the survivor could add a beneficiary designation.

> EXAMPLE: Marilyn and Richard buy Treasury bonds and notes, and hold title to their account as "Marilyn Vanderburg and Richard Vanderburg, with right of survivorship." Many years later, after Marilyn's death, Richard changes the title to add their adult daughter as the beneficiary. Now, the title is held as "Richard Vanderburg, payable on death to Melissa Vanderburg."

Also, you cannot name an alternate beneficiary to inherit the bonds if your first choice does not survive you.

CAUTION

If naming an alternate is important to you, think twice about using the beneficiary form of registration. If you want to name a specific alternate to inherit your government securities without probate, you'll need to use another probate-avoidance method, such as a living trust. (See Chapter 7.) Before you get too concerned, though, weigh several factors, including:

- Your age, and that of your beneficiary. If your primary beneficiary died, do you think you would be able to handle the paperwork to name another beneficiary?
- The value of the securities. If the securities went through probate, would that impose a large expense on whoever inherits them?
- The person you've chosen as your residuary beneficiary of your will. If you're happy with that person as a backup beneficiary, you don't have a problem.

Buying Government Securities

If you want to buy government securities directly, not through a broker, you can do so online at www.treasurydirect.gov, which also offers lots of information about savings bonds and treasury securities.

You can also contact a Federal Reserve Bank servicing office. Every large city has one, as do a fair number of medium-sized cities.

Ask for a Treasury Direct Tender package. It should contain a booklet called *Buying Treasury Securities* and copies of the forms you need.

Name a Beneficiary for Your Vehicles

Transfer-on-Death Registration 72

How It Works.. 73

If You Change Your Mind... 74

Transferring Title After Death 75

Joint Ownership With the Right of Survivorship 75

Special Transfer Procedures for Vehicles... 77

Probate is spectacularly unsuited to cars and other vehicles. Given their maintenance requirements and rapid depreciation, it makes absolutely no sense to have them sitting around for months or years while probate grinds on, before they can be transferred to their new owners.

This chapter discusses a few ways to make sure that a car will get to the person you want to inherit it quickly and easily, without formal probate proceedings.

Transfer-on-Death Registration

So far, only a few states offer car owners the sensible option of naming a beneficiary, right on the car title, to inherit the vehicle. The practice is spreading, though; it's a simple, effective way for folks to pass on their cars, trucks, and small boats.

Beneficiary Registration at a Glance	
Pros	**Cons**
• Easy and free to set up. • You can change your mind at any time.	• Can't name an alternate beneficiary. • Not available in most states.

States With Transfer-on-Death Vehicle Registration		
Arizona	Illinois	Nebraska
Arkansas	Indiana	Nevada
California	Kansas	Ohio
Connecticut	Missouri	Vermont
Delaware		
If you want to look up your state's law, you can find the citation on your state's page in the appendix.		

How It Works

The process is simplicity itself. All you do is apply for a certificate of car ownership in "beneficiary form." The fee is the same as for a standard certificate. The new certificate lists the name of the beneficiary (or more than one), who will automatically own the vehicle after your death.

The beneficiary you name has no rights as long as you are alive. You are free to sell or give away the car, or name someone else as the beneficiary.

In Arizona, Arkansas, Delaware, Kansas, Missouri, Nebraska, Nevada and Vermont, if you own the vehicle with someone else—say, your spouse—you can still designate a beneficiary. The beneficiary will inherit the vehicle only after both you and the other owner have died. In California, Connecticut, Illinois, Indiana, and Ohio, however, transfer-on-death registration is limited to one owner. (And in Illinois, you can't designate a TOD beneficiary if there is a lien on the car—you must own it free and clear.) So you may want to own the vehicle in joint tenancy with the other owner now, which will avoid probate at the first owner's death. Then the sole surviving owner can designate a beneficiary to inherit the car without probate.

Avoiding Probate for Small Boats

In California, Indiana, and Ohio, the beneficiary form of registration is also available for small boats. (Cal. Veh. Code § 9852.7; Ind. Code § 9-31-2-30; Ohio Rev. Code Ann. § 2131.13.) The rules are generally the same as those that apply to other motor vehicles.

TIP

In a community property state, get your spouse's (or registered domestic partner's) consent before naming someone else as beneficiary. In a community property state, your spouse may own a half interest in a vehicle even if it's registered in your name. If you bought it with money you earned while married (or in a registered domestic partnership), it's "community property," and you and your mate own it 50-50 unless you have both signed a written agreement to the contrary.

If the vehicle is community property, and you want to name someone other than your spouse as the beneficiary, get your spouse's written consent—and store it with your title slips and other important documents where they can be found after your death.

If You Change Your Mind

You are free to revoke a beneficiary designation at any time, but there are restrictions on how you can do it. Only two ways, in fact, are allowed. You can either:

- sell the vehicle, or
- apply for a new certificate of ownership, one that does not name a beneficiary at all or names a different one.

You cannot revoke the beneficiary provision by leaving the car to someone else in your will or living trust. If you try, your efforts won't have any effect.

> **EXAMPLE:** Claudia, a Californian, registers her car in beneficiary form, naming her niece Arlene to inherit it. Later, after the two have a falling-out, Claudia writes a will leaving the car to her friend Hal. At Claudia's death, the car will belong to Arlene, despite the will provision to the contrary.

Transferring Title After Death

When the owner dies, the vehicle belongs to the beneficiary listed on the certificate of ownership. To re-title the vehicle in his or her own name, the new owner must submit to the state motor vehicles agency several documents:

- an application for the new certificate
- the old certificate of ownership, if available, and
- a death certificate to prove that the former owner has died.

Once the new owner turns in these documents and pays the required fee, the state agency will issue a new certificate of ownership.

The beneficiary inherits any outstanding debts on the vehicle, as well as the vehicle. So if your car isn't paid off at your death, the beneficiary will inherit your obligation to repay the loan.

Joint Ownership With the Right of Survivorship

If you're part of a couple—married or not—it's often smart to hold title to your cars together, as "joint tenants with the right of survivorship." That way, when one owner dies, the other will own the vehicle, without probate.

In some states (Oregon, for example), you don't have to add any magic words to the title document: If you own a car jointly with someone else, and one of you dies, the survivor automatically owns the car. In Kentucky, that's true only if the co-owners are husband and wife.

In most states, however, you must take some care to set up the ownership in a way that will let the survivor inherit the car without probate. Usually, the car registration document must spell out that you own the car "in joint tenancy with right of survivorship." When you go to register your car, your state's motor vehicles agency should be able to tell you what words to use to achieve the result you want. Texas includes on its certificates of title a "Rights of Survivorship Agreement Form" for husbands and wives to sign.

After one owner dies, the surviving owner automatically owns the vehicle. But the new sole owner must still reregister title in his or her name alone. This process is sometimes called clearing title. Usually, it's quite easy; all that the state motor vehicles department requires is a written statement from the new owner (the state may provide a fill-in-the-blanks form) and proof of death (a death certificate). Some states issue a new certificate of ownership for free in these circumstances.

CAUTION

Be cautious about adding a co-owner just to avoid probate. Many single, older people are tempted to make someone—a grown son or daughter, perhaps—the joint owner of a car, solely for the purpose of avoiding probate. But in many instances, that's not a good idea. Keep in mind that you're giving away a half interest in the car, which can have several undesirable consequences:

- If you change your mind, you can't get the half interest back unless the other co-owner agrees; a gift is permanent.
- If the co-owner is on the losing end of a lawsuit or files for bankruptcy, a creditor could seize his or her interest in the car.
- If the half interest is worth more than the amount of the annual federal gift tax exclusion ($14,000 in 2014), you are required to file a federal gift tax return. No gift tax will actually be due, however, unless at your death you have given away or left such a large amount of property that you have exceeded the gift and estate tax threshold, as explained in Chapter 9. (And given how quickly new cars plummet in value after they're driven off the dealer's lot, gift tax should be a concern only if you're sharing a spanking new car.)

(Joint tenancy is discussed further in Chapter 6.)

Special Transfer Procedures for Vehicles

Even if your state doesn't let you register vehicles in transfer-on-death form, and you don't own it in joint tenancy, the person who inherits your car—through your will, for example—may still be able to take title to it without probate court proceedings.

It depends on where you live. Some states have special nonprobate transfer procedures just for vehicles. All the new owner must do is complete a simple written statement (affidavit) setting out some basic facts, sign it in front of a notary public, and file it with the state agency that registers vehicles. For example, in Hawaii, a vehicle, regardless of value, can be transferred to its new owner by affidavit. (Haw. Rev. Stat. § 560:3-1201.) In Utah, up to four vehicles can be transferred this way if the rest of the deceased person's estate is worth $100,000 or less. (Utah Code Ann. § 75-3-1201.)

But in many states, there's an important restriction: The affidavit procedure is available only if probate isn't necessary for any of your other assets. If a regular probate proceeding is going on, the car must go through that process. If you want to know the specifics of your state's paperwork, contact a local office of the state motor vehicles agency.

> EXAMPLE: Graham, an Oregon resident, dies owning a house, a car, several mutual fund accounts, a bank account, an individual retirement account (IRA), and some household furnishings and personal belongings.
>
> Before his death, Graham named pay-on-death beneficiaries for his mutual fund accounts and IRA. He and his wife held their house in tenancy by the entirety and a bank account in joint tenancy with right of survivorship. In his will, he left his personal belongings to his wife and his car to his son.
>
> Whether or not the car qualifies for the affidavit procedure depends on whether probate is required for the rest of Graham's estate. Here's how it breaks down:

Asset	Probate necessary?
House	No, because owned in tenancy by the entirety with his wife
Personal belongings	No, because value isn't high enough to necessitate probate under Oregon law
IRA, mutual funds	No, because Graham named pay-on-death beneficiary
Bank account	No, because held in joint tenancy with right of survivorship with his wife
Car	No, because probate is not necessary for any other property. Graham's son can file a simple form with the state Motor Vehicles Division and immediately take title to the car.

If the simplified procedure is available, your state's motor vehicles department may provide a form (at its offices and online) for the inheritors to fill out and file. The Oregon affidavit form is shown below.

If there isn't an official form, the person who inherits a vehicle will have to write up an affidavit (a sworn statement, signed in front of a notary public), including whatever information the state law then requires. For example, the affidavit might need to state that no probate proceedings are underway or planned, and list all the known heirs of the deceased person.

Finding out exactly what's required in the affidavit may require looking up the state statute that sets out the specific requirements. You can find your state's statutes at any public law library (available in most courthouses) or online. To look up a statute online, start at the part of the Nolo website, www.nolo.com/legal-research/state-law.html, that links to all states' statutes. If you're lucky, your state's website will offer you a table of contents. Start here and look for the

Sample Oregon Form

DMV
DEPARTMENT OF TRANSPORTATION
DRIVER AND MOTOR VEHICLE SERVICES
1905 LANA AVE NE, SALEM OR 97314

INHERITANCE AFFIDAVIT

If a deceased owner's estate is not probated, their interest in a vehicle may be assigned through the use of this affidavit signed by all the heirs of the owner(s) stating the name of the person to whom the ownership interest has been assigned. (ORS 803.094)

This form must be completed by the heir(s) and submitted to DMV with the title (if available), application for title, and title transfer fee.

- **DMV must receive an affidavit completed and signed by all heirs.** Heirs are determined according to ORS Chapter 112. DMV cannot determine the heirs for you. You may wish to seek legal counsel to determine who the heirs are.

- If there is more than one heir, the heirs may either complete and sign the same affidavit or complete and sign separate affidavits. Each affidavit must indicate to whom ownership of the vehicle is assigned.

- If there are no other heirs, leave the space provided below for listing heirs blank.

- If the heir is a minor or is incapacitated, the parent or guardian must sign for the heir. (Example: Jane Q. Public, age 10, by *John Q. Public*, parent.) If the guardian signs, a copy of the court papers showing guardianship must be submitted with the affidavit.

- The affidavit must be signed before a notary. (The notary does not have to be from the State of Oregon.)

I/We, _____

declare that _____

died on the _____ day of _____ , 20 _____ ; and that the estate has not

and will not be probated.

At the time of death, the deceased was the owner of the following described vehicle:

PLATE NUMBER	YEAR	MAKE	VEHICLE IDENTIFICATION NUMBER

List all heirs. (Any heirs not signing this affidavit must complete a separate affidavit.) **I certify if there are no names listed below, there are no other heirs.**

I/we release any and all claim to the following party:

NAME OF PERSON TO WHOM OWNERSHIP OF THE VEHICLE HAS BEEN ASSIGNED.	ADDRESS	
CITY	STATE	ZIP CODE

ALL HEIRS MUST SIGN BELOW

SIGNATURE OF HEIR	SIGNATURE OF HEIR
X	X
SIGNATURE OF HEIR	SIGNATURE OF HEIR
X	X

NOTARY

State of _____ County of _____

Subscribed and sworn before me this _____ day of _____ , 20 ___

by _____ .

X _____
SIGNATURE OF NOTARY PUBLIC

735-516 (1-13) STK# 300165

sections about vehicles or probate. If that's not available, you can probably search for a particular word.

Some states charge the regular fee to issue a new certificate of ownership; others do it for free.

Where Spouses Have It Easy

In Maine, if a married person dies owning any vehicles registered in that state, they automatically pass to the surviving spouse unless a will provides otherwise (or someone who has a legal claim on the car, such as a loan company, refuses to consent). Registration and title are transferred to the surviving spouse with no fee or tax. (Me. Rev. Stat. Ann. tit. 29-A, § 663.)

In Ohio, a surviving spouse automatically gets up to two cars, without probate, unless the deceased spouse left them to someone else by will or TOD registration. (Ohio Rev. Code § 2106.18.)

Michigan also has a special rule for spouses. A surviving spouse (or heir if there is no spouse and no will) can claim a vehicle without probate if:

- the deceased spouse left vehicles with a total value of less than $60,000, and
- no other assets require regular probate.

The spouse applies to the Michigan Secretary of State for a new title. (Mich. Comp. Laws Ann. § 257.236.)

These are just examples. You may want to check your own state's laws for procedures your family could take advantage of.

TIP

Don't overlook simple procedures for small estates. Even if your state does not have a special transfer procedure just for vehicles, your inheritors may still be able to transfer a vehicle—and everything else you leave—without probate if the value of your estate is small enough. (See Chapter 8.)

Name a Beneficiary for Your Real Estate

Can You Use a TOD Deed? 82

How It Works: An Overview 83

Possible Drawbacks of TOD Deeds 85

    Effect on Medicaid Eligibility 85

    No Quick Sale After Death 85

How to Prepare, Sign, and Record the Deed 86

    Get a Deed Form or Prepare Your Own 86

    Name the Beneficiary 87

    Describe the Property 87

    Sign the Deed 87

    Record the Deed 88

Three Ways to Cancel the Deed—And One Way Not To 90

    Record a Revocation 90

    Record a New TOD Deed 92

    Transfer the Property to Someone Else 92

How the New Owner Claims the Property 92

For most homeowners, keeping a house out of probate is their biggest probate-avoidance wish—and challenge. A living trust works well, but not everyone wants to go to the expense and trouble of creating one. And joint tenancy isn't always the best option, either. Here's good news: More and more states are now offering an easy and effective alternative for real estate within their borders, and other states are considering adopting it.

This alternative is called a transfer-on-death deed or beneficiary deed in most states. It's like a regular deed used to transfer real estate, with a crucial difference: It doesn't take effect until your death.

Transfer-on-Death Deeds at a Glance	
Pros	**Cons**
• Easy to create, usually. • You can change your mind at any time. • After your death, easy for beneficiary to transfer title.	• You may need a lawyer to help you prepare a deed valid in your state.

Can You Use a TOD Deed?

If you own real estate in any of the states listed below, you can use a TOD deed to leave that real estate to someone. No other states allow these kinds of deeds yet.

If you try to leave property in another state by deed at your death, it won't work. For example, if you sign a deed transferring your house to your children and stick it in your desk drawer, knowing that they will find it there after your death, the deed won't have any effect. A deed is not a valid substitute for a will (which must be signed in front of witnesses) unless state law specifically allows it.

States with Transfer-on-Death Deeds	
Arizona	Beneficiary deed
Arkansas	Beneficiary deed
Colorado	Beneficiary deed
District of Columbia	Transfer-on-death deed
Hawaii	Transfer-on-death deed
Illinois	Transfer-on-death instrument
Indiana	Transfer-on-death deed
Kansas	Transfer-on-death deed
Minnesota	Transfer-on-death deed
Missouri	Beneficiary deed
Montana	Beneficiary deed
Nebraska	Transfer-on-death deed
Nevada	Deed upon death
New Mexico	Transfer-on-death deed
North Dakota	Transfer-on-death deed
Ohio	Transfer-on-death designation affidavit
Oklahoma	Transfer-on-death deed
Oregon	Transfer-on-death deed
Virginia	Transfer-on-death deed
Wisconsin	Transfer-on-death deed
Wyoming	Transfer-on-death deed

How It Works: An Overview

Using a transfer-on-death deed is a lot like using a payable-on-death designation for a bank account. You name one or more beneficiaries now, who then inherit the property at your death without the need for probate court proceedings.

To name a beneficiary, you use a special kind of deed, one that's tailored to the law of your state. The deed looks pretty much like any other real estate deed; it shows who owns the property, who it's being transferred to, and describes the property exactly. But a TOD deed contains an additional statement, making it clear that the deed does not take effect until the current owner's death. A sample deed, from Colorado, is shown later in this chapter.

The beneficiary you name to inherit the property doesn't have any legal right to it until your death—or, if you own the property with your spouse or someone else, until the last surviving owner dies. The beneficiary doesn't have to sign, acknowledge, or even be told about the deed.

In the deed, you can also name an alternate beneficiary who will inherit the real estate if your first choice isn't alive at your death. If you don't name an alternate, and your first choice doesn't survive you, state law determines who will inherit the property.

After you've signed the deed, you must record it with the local county land records office before your death. Otherwise, it won't be valid.

You keep complete ownership of and control over the property while you're alive. You pay the taxes on it, and it's not protected from your creditors. You can sell it, give it away, or mortgage it. Because the TOD deed does not make a gift of the property, there's no need to concern yourself with gift tax.

Later, if you change your mind about who you want to inherit the property, you are not locked in. You can revoke the TOD deed or simply record another TOD deed leaving the property to someone else.

At your death, ownership passes immediately—and automatically—to the beneficiary you named in the deed. Any mortgage or debt attached to the land goes along with it. The new owner will, at most, have to record a sworn statement (affidavit) and a copy of the death certificate. The process is definitely much simpler and quicker than probate.

⊘ **CAUTION**
Watch out for your state's special rules. Every state has its own rules about TOD deeds, and some of these may be important. Before you set off to prepare your deed, read your state's statute yourself (see below for a tip on how to find it) or consult a knowledgeable lawyer—or do both.

Possible Drawbacks of TOD Deeds

Using a transfer-on-death deed can have important unintended consequences.

Effect on Medicaid Eligibility

Using a TOD deed may temporarily interfere with your eligibility to receive Medicaid benefits. Medicaid is the federal program, administered and partly paid for by the states, that provides medical benefits based on financial need. Because you still own property that you've made subject to a TOD deed, the property is still counted as one of your assets for purposes of Medicaid eligibility. After a Medicaid recipient's death, the state may seek reimbursement from the person's assets—including property left through a TOD deed— for amounts the state spent on the person's medical care.

In some states (Colorado for one), having recorded a TOD deed makes you ineligible for Medicaid. Fortunately, it is easy to solve this problem if you someday want to apply for Medicaid. All you have to do is revoke the deed. (How to revoke is discussed below.)

No Quick Sale After Death

A TOD deed may not be the best choice if you think the property will need to be sold very soon after your death. That's because creditors always have a few months in which to make claims against the property. (In Oregon, they have 18 months.) Creditors can also make claims if the property goes through probate, but the executor would still probably be able to sell the property.

As a practical matter, though, a delay of a few months isn't usually going to matter. It takes a while to sell a house, and inheritors probably won't want to rush into a transaction anyway.

How to Prepare, Sign, and Record the Deed

If your deed doesn't contain the right language, isn't formatted in the correct way, or isn't notarized properly, it won't work. A deed is a simple, one-page document, and it isn't hard to get it right—you just have to pay close attention to your state's requirements.

Get a Deed Form or Prepare Your Own

You can buy a fill-in-the-blanks deed form or type up your own document. State-specific TOD deed forms are available online and in some office supply stores. Be sure any form you use meets the requirements of your state's TOD deed statute. Many of these statutes specify just what language the deed must contain.

RESOURCE

Finding your state's statute. You can find the most recent version of your state's statute online, using the citation on your state's page in the appendix. Start at www.nolo.com/legal-research/state-law.html.

State-specific forms. You can purchase a TOD deed form for your state at www.nolo.com.

You must also format the deed so that it will be acceptable for recording in the local land records office. For example, you'll have to leave a certain amount of space at the top of the page for the recording information that the clerk will add to the document. You can find out all the requirements from the recording office ahead of time.

Name the Beneficiary

You can name anyone you please to inherit your real estate—a person, more than one person, or an organization such as a favorite charity. Your choice is called the "grantee-beneficiary" in most states. You can also name an alternate beneficiary, commonly called a "successor grantee-beneficiary."

Name each beneficiary specifically; don't use categories such as "my nieces and nephews." If you want to leave your house to your two children, then on the deed you should put, for example, "Robert P. Wyman and Rosamund M. Wyman," not "my children." In some states a deed left to a category of beneficiaries simply isn't valid; in others, it will be confusing at best.

If you name more than one beneficiary, you can choose how they will take title to the property. For example, you may want to leave it to them "as joint tenants," meaning that when one dies, the surviving co-owners will automatically own the property. But each state has its own options—for example, a few states don't recognize the term "joint tenants." If the beneficiaries want a different arrangement, they can change the way they hold title once they own the property.

Describe the Property

Copy the exact description of the property—carefully—from your current deed. Then check it over at least once.

Sign the Deed

If you own the property alone, you're probably the only person who needs to sign the deed.

There's one exception: If you live in a community property state, both you and your spouse should sign the deed, just to make it clear that your spouse doesn't object.

> **CAUTION**
> **If you think your spouse might revoke the deed later, see a lawyer.** If you have any reason to think that if you died first, your spouse would revoke the transfer-on-death deed, frustrating your wish to have it go to the TOD beneficiary, see a lawyer before you prepare a TOD deed.

If you own the property with someone else, you should both sign the deed. The TOD deed will not take effect until the last surviving owner dies.

> **EXAMPLE:** Jack and Maureen own their house together as joint tenants, which means that when one of them dies, the survivor will automatically own the property. They sign and record a TOD deed, leaving the property to their adult son Ryan at their death. After Jack dies, Maureen owns the property alone. At her death, it goes to Ryan.

If only one co-owner signs a TOD deed, it will have no effect unless that co-owner is the last surviving owner.

Notarization. You must sign the deed in front of a notary public. That means you need a notarization statement (commonly called an "acknowledgment") at the bottom of the deed, which the notary will fill in and sign.

Witnesses. In some states, including Illinois, Nebraska, and Oklahoma, the deed must also be signed by two witnesses, and their signatures must be notarized as well.

Record the Deed

Your deed won't be effective unless it's recorded (filed) in the local public records before your death. It's always a good idea to record the deed promptly, and some states may require it. Nebraska, for example, requires a TOD deed to be recorded within 30 days after it's executed. (Neb. Rev. Stat. § 76-3410.) To get that done, take the signed deed to the land records office for the county in which

Sample Transfer-on-Death Deed (Colorado)

Recording requested by:	
And when recorded mail this deed and tax statements to:	
	For recorder's use

Beneficiary Deed

(§§ 15-15-401, ET SEQ., Colorado Revised Statutes)

CAUTION: THIS DEED MUST BE RECORDED PRIOR TO THE DEATH OF THE GRANTOR IN ORDER TO BE EFFECTIVE.

_____ *(Name of grantor)* _____ , as grantor,

designates _____ *(Name of grantee-beneficiary)* _____

as grantee-beneficiary whose address is _____

_____

(Note to Assessor and Treasurer: This address is for identification purposes only, all notices and tax statements should continue to be sent to grantor.)

(Optional)[or if grantee-beneficiary fails to survive grantor, grantor designates _____

_____ *(Name of successor grantee-beneficiary)* _____ , as successor

grantee-beneficiary whose address is _____]

and grantor transfers, sells, and conveys on grantor's death to the grantee-beneficiary, the following

described real property located in the County of _____ , State of Colorado:

(insert legal description here)

Known and numbered as _____

THIS BENEFICIARY DEED IS REVOCABLE. IT DOES NOT TRANSFER ANY OWNERSHIP UNTIL THE DEATH OF THE GRANTOR. IT REVOKES ALL PRIOR BENEFICIARY DEEDS BY THIS GRANTOR FOR THIS REAL PROPERTY EVEN IF THIS BENEFICIARY DEED FAILS TO CONVEY ALL OF THE GRANTOR'S INTEREST IN THIS REAL PROPERTY.

WARNING: EXECUTION OF THIS BENEFICIARY DEED MAY DISQUALIFY THE GRANTOR FROM BEING DETERMINED ELIGIBLE FOR, OR FROM RECEIVING MEDICAID UNDER TITLE 26, COLORADO REVISED STATUTES.

WARNING: EXECUTION OF THIS BENEFICIARY DEED MAY NOT AVOID PROBATE.

Executed this _____ *(Date)* _____ .

_____

(Grantor)

[Notarization]

the real estate is located. This office is commonly called the county recorder, land registry, or registrar of deeds. If you aren't sure, call the courthouse and ask where to record deeds.

You'll have to pay a small fee for recording. The clerk will stamp some recording information on the deed, make a copy for the public records, and return the original to you.

Three Ways to Cancel the Deed— And One Way Not To

You can always change your mind after you record a TOD deed. The beneficiary has absolutely no rights over the property until after your death.

But first, a caution: Don't use your will to try to revoke a transfer-on-death deed. It won't work.

> EXAMPLE: Betty records a TOD deed leaving her house to her niece Emily, who has been a great help to her during a serious illness. In her will, she leaves everything else to her son, who lives far away. Years later, when Betty gets around to revising her will, she decides that her son should inherit the house after all. In her will, she states that he is to inherit the house.
>
> When Betty dies, Emily will automatically own the house, despite what the will says. The will has no effect on the recorded deed.

Record a Revocation

The clearest way to make your intention clear is to sign a simple document revoking the TOD deed and record it just like you recorded the original deed. Then the public records show that the deed was revoked. A sample revocation (taken from the Arkansas statute) is shown below.

Generally, all co-owners will want to sign the revocation. If you own the property with someone else and you all have the right of survivorship, the revocation isn't effective unless it's signed by the last surviving owner.

> **EXAMPLE:** Joyce and Eric own their house in tenancy by the entirety, which gives each of them the right of survivorship. They sign and record a TOD deed leaving the house to their daughter. Later, Joyce records a revocation. If she dies first, Eric will be the sole owner. Because he didn't sign the revocation, it will have no effect, and their daughter will own the property when Eric dies.

Sample Revocation of Transfer-on-Death Deed (Arkansas)

Revocation of BENEFICIARY DEED

CAUTION: THIS REVOCATION MUST BE RECORDED PRIOR TO THE DEATH OF THE GRANTOR IN ORDER TO BE EFFECTIVE.

The undersigned hereby revokes the beneficiary deed recorded on July 19, 20xx, instrument number 3388449, records of Lane County, Arkansas.

Date: _____ *September 4, 20xx* _____
Signature of grantor(s): _____ *Marilee N. Simmons* _____

[Notarization]

Record a New TOD Deed

You can also simply sign and record a new TOD deed, leaving the property to someone else. Most states' laws specifically say that if there is more than one TOD deed, only the most recent one is valid. It's still clearer, however, to record a revocation and then a new deed.

Transfer the Property to Someone Else

You are free to give away or sell the property that you've left in a TOD deed. If you no longer own the property at your death, the TOD deed will have no effect.

How the New Owner Claims the Property

After the real estate's owner dies, generally, all the TOD beneficiary has to do is file a short sworn statement (affidavit) and the death certificate in the public land records. This establishes a record of when the property changed hands and who the new owner is.

In most states, the affidavit must state the name of the new owner, describe the property, and give the date of the previous owner's death. It may also have to state the value of the property at the date of death. A sample affidavit, from Nevada, is shown below. Remember, however, that the TOD beneficiary should check the state statute or consult a lawyer to find out the exact requirements in effect when the transfer takes place.

Sample Death of Grantor Affidavit (Nevada)

DEATH OF GRANTOR AFFIDAVIT

Madison R. Benjamin, being duly sworn, deposes and says that Julius M. Benjamin, the decedent mentioned in the attached certified copy of the Certificate of Death, is the same person as Julius M. Benjamin, named as the grantor or as one of the grantors in the deed upon death recorded on March 13, 20xx, as document or file number 88889, book 46, at page 235, records of Washoe County, Nevada, covering the real property commonly known as 167 Oak Street, City of Reno, County of Washoe, State of Nevada, and more particularly described as:

(Legal Description)

Madison R. Benjamin is the beneficiary or at least one of the beneficiaries to whom the real property is conveyed upon the death of the grantor Julius M. Benjamin or is the authorized representative of the beneficiary or at least one of the beneficiaries. The beneficiary or beneficiaries listed in the deed upon death is Madison R. Benjamin.

THE UNDERSIGNED HEREBY AFFIRMS THAT THIS DOCUMENT SUBMITTED FOR RECORDING CONTAINS A SOCIAL SECURITY NUMBER OF A PERSON OR PERSONS.

_____
Date

_____
Signature

[Notarization]

Hold Property In Joint Ownership

Kinds of Joint Ownership That Avoid Probate 96

Joint Tenancy 98

    How Joint Tenancy Avoids Probate 99

    Limitations of Joint Tenancy 101

    Drawbacks of Adding a New Joint Tenant Just to Avoid Probate 103

    How to Take Title in Joint Tenancy 107

    Some Special State Requirements for Joint Tenancy Language 108

Tenancy by the Entirety 110

Community Property 112

    Community Property Basics 112

    Community Property With the Right of Survivorship 114

    Community Property Agreements 117

    Regular Community Property 120

Alternatives to Joint Ownership 122

I f you own valuable property with someone else, you may already have a leg up in the probate-avoidance climb. Several forms of joint ownership—joint tenancy, for example—allow you to avoid probate when the first owner dies.

Many couples conclude that holding title to their major assets in a form of joint ownership that avoids probate is all the estate planning they want to engage in, at least while they are younger. The most attractive features of this strategy are its simplicity and economy. To take title with someone else in a way that will avoid probate, you usually don't have to prepare any additional documents. All you do is state, on the paper that shows your ownership (a real estate deed, for example), how you want to hold title. No expense, no lawyers.

When one owner dies, it's easy for the survivor to transfer the property into his or her name alone, without probate. After that, however, the survivor will have to find another method to avoid probate on his or her death.

Kinds of Joint Ownership That Avoid Probate

There are several ways to own property together with someone else, and it's important to realize that not all of these ways avoid probate. The most common forms of co-ownership are listed below. Scan the list to see which of the probate-avoidance options may be available to you; each one is discussed in detail later in the chapter.

You and your mate may already own your house, joint bank accounts, or other valuable property in a way that will avoid probate when one of you dies. When title and escrow companies prepare real estate deeds, it's a common practice for them to list the new owners as joint tenants or, if they're married, as tenants by the entirety, unless directed otherwise.

Joint Ownership Methods	
Method of Holding Title	**Avoids Probate?**
Joint tenancy with right of survivorship	Yes
Tenancy by the entirety*	Yes
Community property* (Alaska, Arizona, California, Idaho, Louisiana, Nevada, New Mexico, Texas, Washington, Wisconsin)	No, except in states where right of survivorship can be added
Community property with right of survivorship* (Alaska, Arizona, California, Idaho, Nevada, Wisconsin)	Yes
Tenancy in common	No
Partnership	No
* Married couples only (or in some states, registered domestic partners); not available in all states	

Not sure just how you hold title? You're not alone. Most people don't pay much attention to how their names are listed on title documents. Fortunately, usually all it takes is a glance at those documents—for example, the deed to your house—to see how you and the other co-owner currently hold title.

If You're Not Sure How You Hold Title	
Kind of Property	**Where to Look**
Real estate	Your deed
Bank account	The passbook, or the registration card on file at the bank
Brokerage account	A statement for the account
Car, boat, or other vehicle	Certificate of ownership (title) or registration slip
Individual stocks or bonds	Stock certificates or bonds

Joint Tenancy

Joint tenancy is unquestionably the most popular probate-avoidance device around. And why not? Property owned in joint tenancy automatically passes, without probate, to the surviving owner(s) when one owner dies. Setting up a joint tenancy is easy and it doesn't cost a penny.

Joint tenancy often works well when couples (married or not) acquire real estate, vehicles, bank accounts, securities, or other valuable property together. There can be, however, some serious drawbacks (discussed below), especially if you own property by yourself and are thinking of making someone else a joint tenant just to avoid probate.

In many states, married couples often take title not in joint tenancy, but in "tenancy by the entirety" instead. It's very similar to joint tenancy, but is limited to married couples only. (In states that give registered domestic partners or civil union partners the same rights as married couples, however, those couples can also own property as tenants by the entirety.) Both avoid probate in exactly the same way. If you're married and interested in tenancy by the entirety, read this section first for the general joint tenancy rules; then check the discussion of tenancy by the entirety, below.

Joint Tenancy at a Glance	
Pros	**Cons**
• It's easy to create. • It's easy for the survivor to transfer title to himself or herself after one owner dies. • It works for just about anything you own: cars, real estate, bank accounts, stocks, and more. • The survivor may not have to worry about creditors' claims. After one owner dies, joint tenancy property may be subject only to claims for debts that are the joint responsibility of both joint tenants. • You can have two or more joint tenants.	• The last surviving joint tenant must use another method to avoid probate at his or her death. • Probate is not avoided if both owners die simultaneously (a very unlikely event). • Share of each owner must be equal (except in Colorado, Connecticut, North Carolina, Ohio, or Vermont). • Not available for some kinds of property in some states. • If you own property by yourself, adding a joint tenant requires making a gift of a half interest in the property.

How Joint Tenancy Avoids Probate

When one joint owner (called a joint tenant, though it has nothing to do with renting) dies, the surviving joint owners automatically get the deceased owner's share of the joint tenancy property. This automatic transfer to the survivors is called the "right of survivorship." The property doesn't go through probate court—the survivor(s) need only shuffle some simple paperwork to get the property into their names.

The exact steps depend on the type of property, but generally all the new owner has to do is fill out a straightforward form and present it, with a death certificate, to the keeper of ownership records: a bank, state motor vehicles department, or county real estate records office.

> **EXAMPLE:** Evelyn and her daughter Miya own a car together, registered in their names as joint tenants with right of survivorship. When Evelyn dies, her half interest in the car will go to her daughter without probate. To get the car registered in her name alone, Miya will need only to fill out a simple form and file it with the state motor vehicles agency.

If you're a joint tenant, you cannot leave your share to anyone other than the surviving joint tenants. So even if your will specifically leaves your half interest in a joint tenancy car or house to someone else, the will has no effect. The surviving joint tenant will automatically own the property after your death.

But this rule is less ironclad than it may sound. In most circumstances, a joint tenant can easily, and unilaterally, break the joint tenancy at any time before death.

> **EXAMPLE:** Eleanor and Sadie own a house together as joint tenants. Without telling Sadie, Eleanor signs a deed (and records it in the county land records office) transferring her half interest from herself as a joint tenant to herself as a "tenant in common." (Tenancy in common is a form of co-ownership that does not include the right of survivorship.) This ends the joint

tenancy, leaving Eleanor free to leave her half interest in the property to someone else in her will.

In theory, you could also end a joint tenancy by transferring your share of the property to someone else. But this is unlikely, because very few outsiders want to buy into a co-ownership with a stranger. You could, however, give your share to someone, or a creditor may go after it. If a joint tenant does transfer a share of property to a new owner, that new owner isn't a joint tenant with the other original owners. Instead, they are "tenants in common," a form of ownership that does not carry with it the right of survivorship.

EXAMPLE 1: Sean and Alice own a beach house, which they inherited from their parents, in joint tenancy. Sean gives his half interest to his grown children, making them tenants in common with Alice. When Alice dies, her interest will *not* automatically go to Sean's children. Instead, it will pass under the terms of her will.

EXAMPLE 2: Don, Melanie, and Barbara own property together in joint tenancy. Don deeds his one-third interest to Josh, his son. Josh is not a joint tenant with Melanie and Barbara; he is a tenant in common, free to leave his property to whomever he wants. Melanie and Barbara, however, are still joint tenants with respect to their two thirds of the property; when one of them dies, the other will own a two-thirds share.

Limitations of Joint Tenancy

There are definite limits on the effectiveness of joint ownership as a probate-avoidance strategy. Most of these drawbacks are of greatest concern to older folks.

Probate is not avoided when the last owner dies. One drawback is obvious: The probate-avoidance part of joint tenancy works only at the death of the first co-owner. (Or, if there are three joint tenants, only at the death of the first two, and so on.) When the last co-owner dies, the property must go through probate before it goes to whomever inherits it, unless the last owner used a different probate-avoidance method, such as transferring the property to a living trust. By contrast, some other probate-avoidance devices, such as living trusts or payable-on-death accounts, let you name a beneficiary who will inherit free of probate when the second co-owner dies.

Probate is not avoided if both owners die simultaneously. In that very unlikely event, each owner's share of the property would pass under the terms of his or her will. If a joint tenant died without a valid will, the property would go to each owner's closest relatives under state law. Either way, probate would probably be necessary.

> **TIP**
>
> **Don't obsess about simultaneous death.** Nolo gets a lot of questions about what happens to joint tenancy property if both members of a couple die in a common disaster. It's a natural concern, but one that shouldn't loom large in your estate planning. Statistically, the chances are almost negligible that co-owners will die at the same time.

One owner's incapacity may hobble the others. Another issue that may concern elderly or ill persons is that if one joint owner became incapacitated and could not make decisions, the other owners' freedom to act would be restricted. This problem can be avoided if each joint owner signs a document called a "durable power of attorney," giving someone authority to manage their affairs if they cannot, or if the property is transferred to a living trust. (See Chapter 7 for information on living trusts.)

Drawbacks of Adding a New Joint Tenant Just to Avoid Probate

Joint tenancy is usually a poor estate planning choice when an older person, seeking only to avoid probate, is tempted to put solely owned property into joint tenancy with someone else. Adding another owner this way creates several potential headaches.

You're giving away property. If you make someone else a joint tenant of property that you now own yourself, you give up half ownership of the property. The new owner could sell or mortgage his or her share—or lose it to creditors or in a divorce.

> EXAMPLE: An Arizona woman and her adult son took title to a condominium as joint tenants. The mother, who had owned the condo with her daughter until then, paid all expenses of the property and received all the income from renting it to tenants.
>
> Later the IRS sued the son for unpaid income taxes, and eventually the condominium was sold to pay the taxes. The mother received half of the proceeds. She sued to get the other half back, arguing that she was the only true owner because the joint tenancy had been created only for estate planning purposes. She lost. If you put property into joint tenancy, the IRS presumes you intend to make a gift, and she could not overcome that legal presumption. (*Nikirk v. U.S.*, 2003 WL 22474742 (D. Ariz. 2003).)

Gift and Estate Taxes

If you create a joint tenancy by making another person a co-owner, federal gift tax may be assessed on the transfer. If gifts to one person (except your spouse) in one year exceed the annual federal gift tax exclusion (currently $14,000), you must file a gift tax return with the IRS. No tax is actually due, however, until you give away a very large amount ($5.34 million for those who die in 2014) in taxable gifts. (See Chapter 9.)

There's one big exception: If two or more people own a bank account in joint tenancy, but one person puts all or most of the money in, no gift tax is assessed against that person. The theory is that because the contributor still has the power to withdraw the money, no gift has been made yet. A taxable gift may be made, however, when the other joint tenant withdraws money from it. (IRS Priv. Ltr. Rul. 94-27003, 1994.)

For federal estate tax purposes, however, you are treated as if you had not given away a part interest in the property. The entire joint tenancy property remains in your taxable estate—the property which, at your death, is subject to federal estate tax. (Most estates don't have to pay estate tax, however, because such a large amount of property is exempt from the tax.) This rule has another consequence as well: At your death, the new owner (the surviving joint tenant) gets a tax basis that is "stepped-up" to the date-of-death value. This can be a valuable tax break for the survivor.

It may spawn disputes after your death. Many older people make the mistake of adding someone as a joint tenant to a bank account just for "convenience." They want someone to help them out by depositing checks and paying bills. But after the original owner dies, the co-owner may claim that he or she is entitled, as a surviving joint tenant, to keep the funds remaining in the account. In some instances, maybe that's what the deceased person really intended—

it's too late to ask. Sadly, this sort of confusion often leads to bitter and permanent family rifts, some of which are fought out in court.

I Remember Mama, and Her Money

A Georgia lawsuit pitted one woman against her siblings, squabbling over their deceased mother's certificates of deposit. The daughter's name had been added to the certificates as a joint owner, and after her mother's death she claimed the money belonged to her.

But the other offspring recalled—and testified at the trial—that the daughter had been the one who suggested the joint-owner arrangement, purportedly to make the money readily available "in case Mama got sick." The jury decided that the joint tenancy had been for convenience only, and that the mother had not intended to make a gift to the daughter. (*Turner v. Mikell*, 195 Ga. App. 766, 395 S.E.2d 20 (1990).)

TIP

Other ways to accomplish your goal. If you just want someone to write checks for you, there are far better ways to do it. If you merely want someone to deposit and write checks for you, consider giving a trusted person a "power of attorney" over some or all of your assets. When you sign a power of attorney, the person you choose, known as your "attorney-in-fact," can act on your behalf—but has no right to the funds in the account. Many banks have their own forms you can use to give someone this limited authority. It's easy to establish or revoke; you don't need a lawyer.

A few states (Florida, Illinois, and Texas, for example) offer the useful option of a "convenience" account. Florida lets a depositor name one or more "agents" who have the right to make deposits, withdraw funds, and write checks on the depositor's behalf. An agent has no rights to the money and doesn't inherit it when the depositor dies.

A surviving spouse may miss an income tax break. If you make your spouse a joint tenant with you on property you own separately, the surviving spouse could miss out on a potentially big income tax break later, when the property is sold.

You need concern yourself with this problem only if:

- you own property separately and want to make your spouse a joint tenant now instead of leaving the property to him or her at your death
- the property's value has gone up (or you expect it to)— something that may happen to real estate or stocks, but not other common property like cars or household goods, and
- you *don't* live in a community property state (Arizona, California, Idaho, Louisiana, Nevada, New Mexico, Texas, Washington, or Wisconsin).

To understand the problem, you need to know a little about IRS "tax basis" rules. The tax basis on any item of property is the amount from which taxable profit is figured when property is sold. Usually, basis is what you paid for the property, with some adjustments. For example, if you buy an antique for $100, that amount is your basis. If, 20 years later, you sell it for $400, IRS rules let you subtract your $100 basis, leaving $300 in taxable profit.

If you own a piece of property by yourself and leave it to your spouse at your death, his or her tax basis is the market value of the property at the time it's inherited. If the value of the property has gone up, the basis goes up (it's "stepped up," in tax jargon), too. That's good, because a higher basis means lower taxable profit when the property is sold.

By contrast, if you transfer the solely owned property to joint tenancy with your spouse, the tax basis of the half you give stays exactly the same; it isn't stepped up. (26 U.S.C. § 2040.)

As noted above, there's a special rule for couples in community property states: Both halves of community property get a stepped-up basis when one spouse dies. This is true even if the community property is held in joint tenancy. But in that case, the surviving spouse must show the IRS that the joint tenancy property was in fact community property—that is, that it was bought with community property funds. If the title documents say joint tenancy, that's what the IRS will go by. You may be better off holding title as community property in the first place, as discussed below.

How to Take Title in Joint Tenancy

Joint tenancy certainly has the virtue of simplicity. To create a joint tenancy, all you need to do is pay attention to the way you and the other co-owners are listed on the title document, such as a deed to real estate, a car's title slip, or the signature card establishing a bank account. In the great majority of states, by calling yourselves "joint tenants with the right of survivorship," or putting the abbreviation "JT WROS" after your names, you create a joint tenancy.

A car salesman or bank staffer may assure you that other words are enough. For example, connecting the names of the owners with the word "or," not "and," does create a joint tenancy, in some circumstances, in some states. But it's always better to unambiguously spell out what you want: joint tenancy with right of survivorship.

> EXAMPLE: When Ken and his wife, Janelle, buy a house, they want to take title in joint tenancy. When the deed that transfers the house to them is prepared, all they need to do is tell the title company to identify them on it this way: "Kenneth J. Hartman and Janelle M. Grubcek as joint tenants with right of survivorship." There should be no extra cost or paperwork.

Joint tenancy is available in all states, although a few impose restrictions, summarized below. Remember that one rule applies in every state except Colorado, Connecticut, North Carolina, Ohio, and Vermont: All joint tenants must own equal shares of the property. If you want a different arrangement, such as 60-40 ownership, joint tenancy is not for you.

State Restrictions on Joint Tenancy	
Alaska	No joint tenancy in real estate, except for husband and wife, who may own as tenants by the entirety
Oregon	Transfer to husband and wife creates tenancy by the entirety unless the document clearly states otherwise
Tennessee	Transfer to husband and wife creates tenancy by the entirety, not joint tenancy
Wisconsin	No joint tenancy between spouses; property becomes survivorship marital property

Some Special State Requirements for Joint Tenancy Language

Especially when it comes to real estate, all law is local, so be sure you know your state's rules on what language is required to create ownership with the right of survivorship. If you're not sure, talk to a local lawyer. Here are just a few special state rules; your state may have its own.

Michigan. Michigan has two forms of joint tenancy. A traditional joint tenancy is formed when property is transferred to two or more persons using the language "as joint tenants and not as tenants in common." Any owner may terminate the joint tenancy unilaterally.

If, however, property is transferred to the new owners using the language "as joint tenants with right of survivorship" or to the new owners "and the survivor of them," the result is different. No owner can destroy this joint tenancy unilaterally. Even if you transfer your interest to someone else, that person takes it subject to the rights of your original co-owner. So if you were to die before your original co-owner, that co-owner would automatically own the whole property.

EXAMPLE: Alice and Ben own land in Michigan as "joint tenants with full right of survivorship." Alice gives her interest to Catherine and dies a few years later, while Ben is still alive. Ben now owns the whole property; Catherine owns nothing.

Oregon. Oregon doesn't use the term "joint tenancy"; instead, you create a survivorship estate. The result is the same as with a joint tenancy: when one owner dies, the surviving owner owns the whole property. But technically, creating a survivorship estate creates what the lawyers call "a tenancy in common in the life estate with cross-contingent remainders in the fee simple." (That clears it up, doesn't it?)

South Carolina. To hold real estate in joint tenancy, the deed should use the words "as joint tenants with rights of survivorship, and not as tenants in common," just to make it crystal clear. (S.C. Code Ann. § 27-7-40.)

Texas. If you want to set up a joint tenancy in Texas, you and the other joint tenants must sign a written agreement. For example, if you want to create a joint tenancy bank account, so that the survivor will get all the funds, specifying your arrangement on the bank's signature card may not be enough. Fortunately, a bank or real estate office should be able to give you a fill-in-the-blanks form.

Take this requirement seriously. A dispute over such an account ended up in the Texas Supreme Court. Two sisters had set up an account together, using a signature card that allowed the survivor to withdraw the funds. But when one sister died, and the other withdrew the funds, the estate of the deceased sister sued—and won the funds—because the signature card's language didn't satisfy the requirements of the Texas statute. (*Stauffer v. Henderson*, 801 S.W.2d 858 (Tex. 1991).) More recently, the Texas Supreme Court ruled that a married couple who owned investment accounts labeled "JT TEN" did have survivorship rights, even though they hadn't signed anything stating whether or not the account had a survivorship feature. (*Holmes v. Beatty*, 290 S.W.3d 852 (Tex. 2009).) But it's still better to be explicit about your intentions.

Tenancy by the Entirety

Tenancy by the entirety is very much like joint tenancy, but it's just for married couples (and in a few states, same-sex partners who have registered with the state). It has almost the same advantages and disadvantages of joint tenancy and is most useful in the same situation: when a couple acquires property together. This form of ownership is available in the states listed below.

States With Tenancy by the Entirety Ownership	
Alaska*	Missouri
Arkansas	New Jersey
Delaware	New York*
District of Columbia	North Carolina*
Florida	Ohio*‡
Hawaii	Oklahoma
Illinois**	Oregon*
Indiana*	Pennsylvania
Kentucky*	Rhode Island*
Maryland	Tennessee
Massachusetts	Vermont
Michigan†	Virginia
Mississippi	Wyoming

* For real estate only
** For homestead property only
† Joint tenancy of husband and wife is automatically a tenancy by the entirety.
‡ Only if created before April 4, 1985

Tenancy by the Entirety	
Pros	**Cons**
• It's easy to create. • It's easy to transfer title to the spouse. • Tenancy by the entirety property is usually subject only to claims for debts that are the joint responsibility of both spouses.	• Probate is avoided only when the first spouse dies. The surviving spouse must use another method. • Probate is not avoided if the spouses die simultaneously (a very unlikely event). • Each spouse must own a half share. • Not available in all states. • In some states, limited to real estate.

There are a few important differences, however, between joint tenancy and tenancy by the entirety. For one, if property is held in tenancy by the entirety, neither spouse can transfer his or her half of the property alone, either while alive or by will or trust. It must go to the surviving spouse. This is different from joint tenancy; a joint tenant is free to break the joint tenancy at any time.

> **EXAMPLE:** Fred and Ethel hold title to their house in tenancy by the entirety. If Fred wanted to sell or give away his half interest in the house, he could not do so without Ethel's signature on the deed.

Other differences may also be important to you. In general, tenancy by the entirety property is better protected than joint tenancy property from creditors of just one spouse. (The rules vary from state to state.) If someone sues one spouse and wins a court judgment, in most states the creditor can't seize and sell tenancy by the entirety property to pay off the debt. And if one spouse files for bankruptcy, creditors can't reach or sever property held in tenancy by the entirety.

Community Property

If you are married (or your state offers registered domestic partnerships or civil unions) and live in a community property state, another way to take title to property with your spouse is available to you: community property. In some states, community property doesn't have to go through probate; in others, it does. You'll have to take a look at your state's rules, discussed below, before you make up your mind about how to hold title. But in states where community property ownership furnishes both probate avoidance and tax benefits after one spouse dies, it may be a better choice than joint tenancy. Tenancy by the entirety is not available in community property states.

Community Property States	
Alaska*	Nevada
Arizona	New Mexico
California	Texas
Idaho	Washington
Louisiana	Wisconsin
* Only if spouses sign a community property agreement	

Community Property Basics

If you live in a community property state, most property acquired by you or your spouse during the marriage is automatically community property, unless you sign an agreement to the contrary. Most important, your earnings are community property, and so is everything you buy with those earnings.

There are important exceptions: Property that one spouse inherits or receives as a gift is not community property. If, however, it gets so mixed with community property that it can no longer be separated—for example, money you inherit is deposited in a joint bank account from which you make withdrawals—it, too, becomes community property.

Each spouse owns a half interest in the community property, and each has equal rights to use and manage it. The consent of both spouses, however, is usually required before the property can be sold or mortgaged.

The law does not require community property go to the surviving spouse when one spouse dies. Each spouse is free to leave his or her half interest in the community property to someone else. (Spouses can change this by the way they hold title to the property, as discussed below.) If community property isn't left to the surviving spouse, probate isn't avoided.

A tax break for the survivor. Community property offers a tax break to the surviving spouse if the property has gone up in value before the first spouse's death. This benefit has to do with tax basis. As explained above, the tax basis is the amount from which taxable profit is figured when property is sold; usually, it's what you paid for the property, with some adjustments.

If you hold property in joint tenancy with your spouse, at your death, only the tax basis of your half of the property is stepped up to its market value at the time of death. The tax basis of the surviving spouse's half stays the same. When the property is later sold, this means higher tax if the property went up in value after the joint tenancy was created but before the first spouse died.

If you hold title to the same property as community property, however—or can prove to the IRS that property held in joint tenancy was actually community property—the tax basis for the whole property is stepped up when one spouse dies. (26 U.S.C. § 1014(b)(6).) That leads to a lower taxable profit if the property is later sold.

> **EXAMPLE:** Hank and Beatrice own their house, which they bought many years ago for $60,000, in community property. When Beatrice dies, the house is worth $130,000. Hank inherits her half interest; his tax basis goes up to $130,000.
>
> If Hank and Beatrice had owned the property in joint tenancy and Hank could not prove to the IRS that it was community property, held in joint tenancy for convenience, his tax basis would be just $95,000 (the $30,000 basis in his half plus the $65,000 basis in her half).

TIP

Joint tenants may not be out of luck. If the surviving spouse can prove to the IRS that the joint tenancy property was actually community property, held in joint tenancy for convenience, he or she can qualify for the favorable tax treatment.

Community Property With the Right of Survivorship

If you live in one of the community property states listed below, you may want to take advantage of an option that lets you avoid probate completely for community property. Those states let couples hold title to property as "community property with right of survivorship"—meaning that when one spouse dies, the other automatically owns the community property.

States Where Couples Can Hold Title as Community Property With Right of Survivorship	
Alaska	Nevada
Arizona	Texas
California	Wisconsin
Idaho	

Community Property With Right of Survivorship at a Glance	
Pros	**Cons**
• It's easy to hold title this way. • It's easy to transfer title to the surviving spouse. • It works for anything a married couple owns: cars, real estate, bank accounts, stocks, and more. • If property goes up in value, the surviving spouse gets an income tax break (compared to holding it in joint tenancy) when the property is sold.	• The surviving spouse must use another method to avoid probate at his or her death (except in Wisconsin; see below). • Probate is not avoided if both spouses die simultaneously (a very unlikely event).

If you hold title this way, the process of transferring title to the surviving spouse is as simple as transferring joint tenancy property. The exact steps depend on the type of property, but generally all the new owner has to do is fill out a straightforward form and present it, with a death certificate, to the keeper of ownership records: a bank, state motor vehicles department, or county real estate records office.

EXAMPLE: Michael and Marla, who live in Nevada, took title to their house as "community property with right of survivorship." After Michael dies, Marla takes his death certificate to the office of the county registrar of deeds. She fills out and files the form provided by that office, which asks her for some basic information about her late husband and the property. When the form is recorded (filed) by the registrar of deeds, it's as good as a probate court order would be as proof that Marla now owns the property.

To turn plain community (or separate) property into right-of-survivorship community property, you simply need to put the right words on the title document, just as you would for joint tenancy property.

Adding the Right of Survivorship to Community Property	
State	**Procedure**
Alaska	Couples take title to property as "survivorship community property."
Arizona	Couples take title to specific property as "community property with right of survivorship."
California	Couples take title to specific property as "community property with right of survivorship."
Idaho	Couples take title to property as "community property with right of survivorship."
Nevada	Couples take title to specific property as "community property with right of survivorship."
Wisconsin	Couples take title to specific property as "survivorship marital property" or sign a marital property agreement (see below).

Spouses are free to change their minds and remove the survivorship provision later, but it must be done in writing. They should prepare a new title document that does not include the right of survivorship.

> **EXAMPLE:** When Liz and her husband Fernando bought their vacation house, they directed the title company to state on the deed to the property that they would own it as community property with right of survivorship.
>
> Years later, they decide that they want Fernando's son, Robert, to inherit his father's half interest in the house. Liz and Fernando sign and record a new deed, changing the way they hold property to plain "community property." In his will, Fernando leaves his half interest to Robert.

A spouse may also be able to act alone to revoke a right of survivorship. In Nevada, a spouse can wipe out the right of survivorship by transferring his or her half-interest in the property. And in Arizona, to remove the right of survivorship from a piece of real estate, either spouse can file a sworn statement, called an "affidavit terminating right of survivorship," with the county recorder in the county where the real estate is located. The state statute sets out what information the affidavit must contain.

Community Property Agreements

In Alaska, Idaho, Texas, Washington, and Wisconsin, a married couple can sign an agreement that will determine what happens to some or all of their property at death. Usually, couples declare all of their property to be community property and leave it to the survivor, without probate, when one spouse dies. In effect, the agreement functions much like a will—with the important difference that the property doesn't have to go through probate when the first spouse dies.

States That Authorize Community Property Agreements	
State	**Statute**
Alaska	Alaska Stat. § 34.77.090
Idaho	Idaho Code § 15-6-201
Texas	Tex. Probate Code Ann. § 451
Washington	Wash. Rev. Code § 26.16.120
Wisconsin	Wis. Stat. Ann. § 766.58

Different states have different rules about what makes community property agreements valid. All states require them to be in writing. They may need to be witnessed or notarized. You may also need to record (file) them in the county where you live and where any real estate that's covered is located.

CAUTION

Be sure you understand what you're doing. If you want to create a community property agreement, be sure to check your state's current rules. If you don't, your agreement may not have the effect you intend.

Another reason for caution is that these agreements are binding contracts. Neither spouse can, acting alone, change or revoke them. To revoke a community property agreement, generally the spouses must:

- agree to cancel (rescind) the agreement
- divorce, or
- separate permanently.

If you and your spouse later run into marital trouble, the agreement will remain in effect unless you agree to revoke it or you get a divorce. Just making a will that leaves your property in a different way may not revoke the agreement.

> **EXAMPLE:** Angeline and her husband, John, who lived in Washington, signed a community property agreement declaring that when one of them died, everything the deceased spouse owned would be converted to community property and would go to the survivor. Later, Angeline and John separated. John filed for legal separation. Angeline made a new will, leaving nothing to John, and died two days later.
>
> A legal fight ensued, with John claiming that the agreement was still valid and so he was entitled to inherit all of Angeline's property. A state appeals court ruled that it would read into the community property agreement a clause that wasn't there but that the spouses would surely have wanted: namely, that the agreement would end if the spouses separated permanently. (*In re Bachmeier*, 106 Wash. App. 862, 25 P.3d 498 (2001).) The Washington Supreme Court reversed the decision, ruling that courts should not imply a provision into an agreement between spouses. Under the statute, only divorce would end the agreement, the court stated. (*Estate of Bachmeier*, 52 P.3d 22 (2002).)

SEE AN EXPERT

Questions? See a lawyer. These rules are mostly determined by courts, and may change. If you have questions about the validity of a community property agreement, or want to revoke one, see a lawyer.

In Alaska and Wisconsin, a community property agreement can name a beneficiary to inherit the property at the *second* spouse's death. (In Washington, some commentators say that this is allowed, but courts have not explicitly said so.) After one spouse dies, however, the survivor can amend the agreement to change who inherits his or her property, unless the agreement expressly forbids it.

EXAMPLE: Julie and Alphonse make a community property agreement. The agreement states that when one of them dies, all of his or her property will go to the surviving spouse. The agreement further states that when the second spouse dies, everything he or she owns will go to Julie's son from a prior marriage.

Julie dies first. Alphonse decides that he doesn't want to leave everything to Julie's son; he wants to leave some money to charity at his death as well. He is free to do so.

Regular Community Property

Of the other community property states, California is the only one to offer significant probate-avoidance for community property that isn't held with the right of survivorship.

California allows regular community property to pass outside of probate via two different procedures. For real estate, the spouse simply files a one-page affidavit (sworn statement) with the county recorder's office. The affidavit states that he or she is entitled to full ownership of the property. For other property, the spouse requests a Spousal Property Order from the probate court, which then authorizes the transfer into the surviving spouse's name.

Idaho offers a simple probate procedure when the surviving spouse didn't leave a will, the entire estate is community property, and the surviving spouse is the only heir. The surviving spouse files a simple petition with the probate court, and the court issues an order stating that the survivor now owns everything.

New Mexico allows a surviving spouse to take title to a home held in community property without probate. But there are several limitations: It's allowed only after a six-month waiting period, only if probate isn't necessary for any other assets, and only if all debts and taxes have been paid.

Washington offers no probate shortcuts for community property. Unless you've signed a community property agreement, community property goes through probate just like everything else.

Regular Community Property (No Right of Survivorship) at a Glance	
Pros	**Cons**
• It's easy to create. • It can apply to anything a couple owns: cars, real estate, bank accounts, stocks, and more. • If property goes up in value, the surviving spouse gets an income tax break (compared to holding it in joint tenancy) when the property is sold.	• NO PROBATE AVOIDANCE except in California. • Even in California, the surviving spouse must use another method to avoid probate at his or her death, and probate is not avoided if both spouses die simultaneously (a very unlikely event).

Obviously, if you live outside California, holding assets as plain community property (with no right of survivorship) doesn't do anything to advance your probate-avoidance planning. For this reason, you may want to hold title to your community property as joint tenancy or put it in a living trust. The property is still, legally, community property, but when one spouse dies, it can be passed to the survivor without probate.

EXAMPLE: Marielle and Arnold live in Idaho. When they buy a house with community property funds (money from their joint bank account), they decide to create a living trust and transfer the house to it. So on the deed that gives them ownership of the property, they list themselves as "Marielle and Arnold

Bruchman, trustees of the Marielle and Arnold Bruchman Revocable Living Trust dated January 31, 20xx."

The house will still be community property, subject to all state community property laws. But when Marielle or Arnold dies, the survivor will be able to transfer the house without probate.

Alternatives to Joint Ownership

If you think that joint ownership isn't for you, you may be casting about for another probate-avoidance method. This book, of course, is full of alternatives. Here are some for a few kinds of assets commonly placed in joint tenancy.

Payable-on-death designations for bank accounts or securities. Adding a beneficiary designation is a simple, free way to avoid probate. See Chapter 1, which discusses payable-on-death bank accounts, and Chapter 3, which explains how to name a beneficiary for securities.

Living trusts for real estate. A living trust is the most flexible alternative for real estate. A trust, unlike joint ownership, allows you to name a beneficiary to inherit the property if the other co-owner dies before you do. And if you transfer the property to a living trust, you will avoid probate both when the first owner dies and when the second one dies. With joint ownership, probate is avoided only when the first owner dies.

Transfer-on-death deeds for real estate. In some states, you can transfer real estate without probate by preparing a deed now that takes effect only at your death. See Chapter 5.

Create a Living Trust

How a Living Trust Avoids Probate 126

    Trust Basics 127

    Who's in Charge 127

    How Property Is Transferred After Your Death 128

Other Advantages of a Living Trust 130

    Protection From Court Challenges 130

    Avoiding a Conservatorship 132

Why You Still Need a Will 133

Do You Really Need a Living Trust? 134

    Your Age and Health 135

    Where You Live 135

    Your Home Life 135

    How Much You Own 136

    What Kind of Assets You Own 136

    How Much You Owe 136

Creating a Valid Living Trust 137

    Writing the Trust Document 138

    Choosing a Successor Trustee... 139

    Leaving Trust Property to Young Beneficiaries 141

    Transferring Property to the Trust 144

What Property to Put in a Trust 145

    Real Estate 146

    Small Business Interests.. 147

Bank Accounts 149

Individual Retirement Accounts 149

Vehicles 149

Property You Buy or Sell Frequently 150

Life Insurance 150

Securities 151

Cash 152

Taxes and Record Keeping 152

Amending or Revoking a Living Trust Document 153

You've probably heard of living trusts, which are also called revocable living trusts or (by lawyers) "inter vivos" trusts. Perhaps you've even been advised—by a lawyer, a newspaper columnist, or your Uncle Harry—that you ought to have one. But if you're like most people, you still have some basic questions: What, exactly, is a living trust? How does it work? And do I really need one?

Living trusts (they're called that just because you create them while you're alive, not in your will) were invented to let people make an end run around probate. Holding your valuable property in trust has virtually no legal consequences while you're alive, because you control the trust. (And you can end it at any time, if you choose to.) But after your death, property held in trust can be easily transferred to the family or friends you left it to—without probate. The terms of the trust document (which is similar to a will) authorize the trustee to make this transfer. Probate courts have no legal authority over property that's held in trust.

As you can see, a living trust performs much the same function as a will. The crucial difference is that property left through a will must go through probate, while property in a living trust can go directly to your inheritors.

Revocable Living Trusts at a Glance	
Pros	**Cons**
• A trust works for anything you own: cars, real estate, bank accounts, stocks, and more.	• A trust is more work to create and maintain than other probate-avoidance devices, because property must be transferred, in writing, to the trustee.
• You can name alternate beneficiaries (unlike many probate-avoidance techniques).	
• You can amend or revoke the trust at any time.	• You may run into hassles if you want to refinance property owned by the trust.
• There is no waiting period after death; property can be transferred to beneficiaries quickly.	• It's unlikely, but in some places, you might have to pay a transfer tax if you put real estate in the trust.
• A trust is harder to attack in court than a will.	
• Spouses can make one combined trust.	
• If you become incapacitated, the successor trustee can take over management of trust property without court authorization.	

How a Living Trust Avoids Probate

A trust can seem like a mysterious creature, dreamed up by lawyers, wrapped in legal jargon, and used for mysterious purposes. But in practice, a standard probate-avoidance trust isn't complicated. Here are the basics.

Trust Basics

The kind of trust that avoids probate is called a revocable living trust. You can create one simply by preparing and signing a document called a declaration (or instrument) of trust. If you and your spouse own valuable property together, you'll probably want to create one trust, together.

The trust document, much like a will, names the people or institutions you want to inherit each item of trust property. One significant advantage of a living trust over simpler probate-avoidance methods is that you can name alternate beneficiaries—people who will inherit if your first choice does not survive you. You can even name alternates for your alternates, if you want an extra layer of contingency planning.

Once you've signed the trust document, you transfer your property—real estate, stocks, bank accounts, whatever—to the trustee, who becomes the legal owner. This step is crucial. If you don't transfer ownership, in writing, to the trustee, the trust document has no effect on what happens to the property at your death.

Holding property in trust has almost no day-to-day effect while you're alive. For all practical purposes, it's as if you still owned it. The property is treated the same way it was before by the government when it assesses income or estate taxes, and by creditors when they are looking to collect on a debt you owe.

Who's in Charge

The trustee is in charge of trust property. You (or you and your spouse, if you create a trust together) are the trustee of your revocable living trust, which means that you keep complete control of all the trust property. As trustee, you can transfer property in and out of the trust, change the beneficiaries you've named, or revoke the trust completely.

EXAMPLE: Ashley Zallon creates a living trust, the Ashley Zallon Revocable Living Trust, and transfers her valuable property—a house and some stocks—into the trust. She names herself as trustee of the trust. As trustee, she can sell, mortgage, or give away the trust property, or take it out of the trust and put it back into her name.

> **TIP**
>
> **You can refinance a mortgage, even if your bank is grumpy about it.** Living trusts are so common these days that banks shouldn't raise an eyebrow if you want to refinance property that's legally held in your name as a trustee instead of as an individual. If your bank or title company does ask questions, it should be reassured if you present a copy of your trust document, which should specifically give you, as trustee, the power to borrow against trust property. In the unlikely event you can't convince a lender to deal with you in your capacity as trustee, find another lender or transfer the property out of the trust and back into your name. Later, after you refinance, you can transfer it back into the living trust.

How Property Is Transferred After Your Death

After you die, the person you named in your trust document to be the "successor trustee" takes over as trustee. He or she is in charge of transferring the trust property to the family, friends, or charities you named as the trust beneficiaries. In most cases, the whole transfer process can be handled within a few weeks at little or no cost.

No probate is necessary for property that was held in trust. For example, if you left real estate in your trust to your son Paul, the successor trustee can simply sign a deed transferring the property from the trust to Paul.

With property like bank accounts or securities, the successor trustee will need to show the institution that he or she has the legal right to take possession of the property. Banks and brokers, which have long experience with living trusts, generally accept the authority of the successor trustee without a fuss after examining a copy of the trust document, with its notarized signature.

Occasionally, however, an institution balks at the idea of releasing a deceased client's money without further proof of authority. It might, for example, demand more proof that the trust is valid or that it hasn't been revoked. In a few instances, institutions have threatened to withhold trust funds until they were shown a "certification" of validity by the lawyer or bank involved in drawing up the trust—even if that was impossible because no lawyer or bank had been involved.

No law requires that a lawyer, broker, or bank be involved with a living trust in any capacity. Requiring the signature of a lawyer or bank is simply a bureaucratic rule, imposed by financial institutions afraid of liability for turning over money to the wrong person. So shaking the money loose will not be an insurmountable problem, even if no lawyer drafted the trust. The successor trustee must simply be persistent. The bank should relent if the successor trustee produces the original, signed and notarized trust document, and offers his or her own notarized statement, stating that the trust is in full force and effect.

When all the trust property has been transferred to the beneficiaries, the living trust ceases to exist.

> **TIP**
> **If you leave property to youngsters, you may want a living trust to continue after your death.** You can arrange for your living trust to stay in existence for a while—even years—after your death. One common reason for doing this is so that property inherited by young beneficiaries can stay in trust, managed by an adult, until they're old enough to handle it on their own. For example, say you want to leave trust property to your young granddaughter. You can direct, in your trust document, that if she is younger than 25 at your death, the property is to stay in trust and be

managed for her by your successor trustee. When she turns 25, she will receive what's left, and the trust will end.

Estate Taxes and Trusts

Like other probate-avoidance devices, a basic living trust has no effect on estate taxes. The taxing authorities don't care whether or not your property goes through probate; all they care about is what you owned at your death. Property you leave in a revocable living trust is still considered part of your estate for federal estate tax purposes.

There are, however, many other kinds of trusts that can save wealthy people money on federal estate taxes. The most common kind of tax-saving trust is the bypass or "AB" trust, which is for couples.

Because bypass trusts can tie up property for a long time, generally they make sense only for older, wealthier couples. For articles that explain AB trusts and other ways to minimize estate tax, see the Estate Tax section of www.nolo.com. And for a thorough discussion of AB trusts, and forms and instructions for preparing one, see *Make Your Own Living Trust*, by Denis Clifford (Nolo.)

Other Advantages of a Living Trust

As you know, the main reason for setting up a revocable living trust is to save your family time and money by avoiding probate. But there are other advantages as well.

Protection From Court Challenges

Court challenges to living trusts, like challenges to wills, are rare. But if there is a lawsuit, it's generally considered more difficult to successfully attack a living trust than a will. That's because your continuing involvement with a living trust after its creation (transferring property in and out of the trust, or making amendments) is evidence that you were competent to manage your affairs.

Someone who wanted to challenge the validity of your living trust would have to bring a lawsuit and prove that:

- when you made the trust, you were mentally incompetent or unduly influenced by someone, or
- the trust document itself is flawed—for example, because the signature was forged.

You needn't concern yourself with the possibility of a lawsuit at all unless you think that a close relative—someone who would inherit from you if you hadn't made the trust or will that you did— might have an ax to grind after your death. Pay attention to certain kinds of simmering family tensions, which sometimes boil over into lawsuits. Here are a few red flags:

- You have children from a previous marriage who don't get along with your current spouse, and either your spouse or the children might feel slighted.
- You are in a relationship—for example, with a gay or lesbian partner—that your closest relatives don't approve of.
- You have a history of mental illness, which might lead relatives to conclude you weren't thinking clearly when you made your trust.
- You don't plan to leave much property to close relatives, and they fear you are being unduly influenced by someone.

CAUTION

See a lawyer if you fear a court battle after your death. If you think relatives might try to turn your estate plan topsy-turvy after your death, talk to an experienced lawyer about how you can bolster your defenses.

Avoiding a Conservatorship

Having a living trust can be extremely useful if you someday become incapable, because of physical or mental illness, of taking care of your financial affairs. This is because if you've made a trust with your spouse or partner, he or she has authority over all the trust property. And if you've made an individual trust, your trust document probably authorizes your successor trustee, whose normal job is to take over as trustee at your death, to step in and manage trust property if you become incapacitated.

This feature of a living trust can be a godsend to family members who are distraught, or quite possibly overwhelmed, by caring for someone who has been struck by a serious illness or accident. Without the authority conferred in a living trust document, family members must usually go to court to get legal authority over the incapacitated person's finances—a painful, public process. Typically, the spouse or adult child of the person asks the court to be appointed as that person's conservator or guardian.

Most trust documents require that before a successor trustee can take charge of trust property, your incapacity would have to be certified in writing by one or two physicians. Once that determination has been properly made, the successor trustee has legal authority to manage all property in the trust, and to use it for your health care, support, and welfare. The law requires him or her to act honestly and prudently.

> **EXAMPLE:** Margaret creates a revocable living trust, appointing herself as trustee. The trust document states that if she becomes incapacitated, and a physician signs a statement saying she no longer can manage her own affairs, her daughter Elizabeth will replace her as trustee. Elizabeth will be responsible for managing trust property and using it for her mother's benefit. At Margaret's death, Elizabeth will distribute the trust property according to the directions in the trust document.

A successor trustee who takes over must also file an annual income tax return for the trust. (As long as you are the trustee of your own trust, no separate trust income tax return is required.)

CAUTION

You should also make a durable power of attorney. Your successor trustee has no authority to manage property outside the trust. And because everyone has, at one time or another, some property that isn't owned by their living trust, it's always a good idea to prepare and sign a document called a durable power of attorney for financial management. In this document, you can authorize your successor trustee to make financial and property management decisions for nontrust property if you become incapacitated.

In addition, if you are concerned about making sure doctors know your wishes about the use of various life-sustaining treatments—not being kept alive artificially, for example—you'll want to prepare and sign some other documents, commonly called a directive to physicians (living will) and durable power of attorney for health care.

RESOURCE

Making the documents. *Quicken WillMaker Plus* software (published by Nolo) creates health care directives and power of attorney forms for every state, and financial durable power of attorney forms.

Why You Still Need a Will

A living trust, powerful as it is, doesn't eliminate the need for a will. There are two main reasons.

One big reason is that a living trust covers only property you have transferred, in writing, to the trust—and almost no one transfers everything to a trust. And even if you do scrupulously try to transfer everything, there's always the chance you'll acquire property shortly before you die. If you don't think to (or aren't able to) transfer ownership of it to your living trust, it won't pass under the terms of the trust document.

Second, a will can do some important things that a living trust document cannot. For example, in many states you must use a will if you have minor children and want to name a guardian—someone to raise them if you and the other parent die before they reach adulthood—for them. You can also use a will to forgive (cancel) debts owed to you, something that isn't done in a trust document.

If you use a living trust as your primary way to leave property, all you need is a bare-bones will. In it, state who should inherit any property that you don't specifically transfer to your living trust or leave to someone in some other way.

One kind of simple will is called a pour-over will, so named because it directs that all your remaining property be poured over into your living trust. That property must still go through probate on the way to your trust, however.

RESOURCE

Making your will. For free information about wills, see the articles in the Wills, Trusts & Estate Planning section of www.nolo.com.

Nolo's Online Will. At www.nolo.com, you can create a will that reflects your wishes and is valid under your state's law. All you need to do is go through an online interview that prompts you to enter all the information needed for a valid will.

Quicken WillMaker Plus. You can also use this Nolo software to make a valid will, as well as other estate planning documents such as powers of attorney and advance medical directives. Lots of legal help guides you through the process.

Do You Really Need a Living Trust?

Although a living trust is undoubtedly the most flexible way to avoid probate, not everyone needs one. Other, simpler probate-avoidance methods may better suit your stage of life. Here are a few factors to consider before you make your decision.

Your Age and Health

If you're young and healthy, your main estate planning goals are probably simple. You want to make sure that in the unlikely event of your early death, your property will go to the people or institutions you want to get it and, if you have young children, that they are well cared for. You don't need a trust to accomplish those ends. Writing a will (in which you name a guardian to raise the children), and perhaps buying some life insurance, would be easier, because a will is simpler to create than a living trust. Later in life, when you're in your 50s or 60s, you can set up a trust.

Where You Live

In some states, probate isn't such a big deal. If your state has streamlined its probate procedures to cut down on expense and delay, maybe you don't want to incur the up-front cost of a living trust now. But if you live in a high-cost state, such as California, a living trust might save your family a lot of money in the long run.

Your Home Life

The nature of your close relationships will have a big effect on your estate planning.

If you're married or are in a long-term relationship, you probably own many, if not all, of your valuable assets together with your mate. If you hold title in joint tenancy, tenancy by the entirety, or (in some states) community property, the property won't have to go through probate when the first owner dies. You may decide to wait until later to create a trust, which will avoid probate at the second death. (Chapter 6 discusses joint ownership options.)

If you own property by yourself, though, you might want to take a closer look at setting up a living trust.

How Much You Own

Most states allow certain amounts or types of property to be transferred without probate, or by a streamlined court procedure, even if it's left by will. (See Chapter 8.) If your estate is eligible for these simpler procedures, you may not need to go to the trouble of making and maintaining a trust.

And keep in mind that the more you own, the more your estate will owe for probate costs. It may not make sense to create a living trust until you've accumulated more assets.

What Kind of Assets You Own

Although a living trust can handle almost any kind of property, it's better suited to some types than others. ("What Property to Put in a Trust," below, discusses this in detail.)

If your wealth is mostly in the form of real estate, a living trust may be a wise strategy for you. But if your money is in bank, brokerage, or retirement accounts, there are simpler and equally effective methods—for example, naming payable-on-death beneficiaries for each account. These methods don't offer all the features of a living trust—most important, you probably won't be able to name an alternate beneficiary. But especially for younger people, that drawback may be outweighed by ease and convenience. (Chapters 1 through 4 discuss these other methods.)

How Much You Owe

If you have a business that has many creditors, you may want your assets to go through probate, to take advantage of the cutoff period for creditors' claims that probate provides. If creditors don't make their claims by the deadline (in most states, a few months after probate proceedings are begun), they're out of luck. Your inheritors can take your property free of concern that creditors will surface later and attempt to claim a share.

Creating a Valid Living Trust

Setting up a valid living trust isn't difficult or expensive, but it does require a fair amount of paperwork—more, say, than just making a will does.

Living Trust Terms

Someone who sets up a living trust is called a **grantor**, **trustor**, or **settlor**.

The property you transfer to the trust is called, collectively, the **trust property**, **trust principal**, or **trust estate**. (And, of course, there's a Latin version: the trust **corpus**.)

The person who has power over the trust property is called the **trustee**. In most instances, the person who sets up the trust (the grantor) is the original trustee of a living trust. If a married couple creates one shared marital trust, both are trustees.

The person you name to take over as trustee after your death (or, with a shared marital trust, after the death of both spouses) is called the **successor trustee**. The successor trustee's job is to transfer the trust property to the beneficiaries, following the instructions in the Declaration of Trust. The successor trustee may also manage trust property inherited by young beneficiaries.

The people or organizations who inherit the trust property when the grantor dies are called **beneficiaries** of the trust.

For many more definitions, see the glossary of this book or check out Nolo's free *Plain-English Law Dictionary* at www.nolo.com.

Writing the Trust Document

The first step is to create a trust document. Lawyers commonly charge upwards of $1,000 to prepare a living trust, but you can do it yourself if you educate yourself with a good do-it-yourself book or software. (Nolo's living trust products are listed below.)

A trust document, formally known as a Declaration of Trust or trust instrument, is broadly similar to a will. It lists whom you want to inherit items of property. One way in which it differs from a will, however, is that it contains a list of property (usually called a schedule) that the trust owns. Another difference is that you can make a trust with your spouse; wills are normally for only one person.

A trust document should be signed in front of a notary public. You don't need to file it with any court or government office; just keep it in a safe place where the successor trustee will be able to get to it after your death.

RESOURCE

Doing it yourself. Nolo offers several ways to learn about and prepare your own living trust:

- Nolo's Online Living Trust. This online service, at www.nolo.com, lets you easily create a living trust that's tailored to your wishes and your state's law. The question-and-answer format makes it simple to enter all the information needed for a valid trust document.
- *Living Trust Maker* software. You can make a probate-avoidance living trust, either for yourself or together with your spouse, with this easy-to-use software. The legal manual that comes with the program discusses living trusts in depth.
- *Make Your Own Living Trust*, by Denis Clifford. This book explains, step by step, how to create your own living trust. It contains instructions and forms for both a simple probate-avoidance trust and for an estate-tax saving (AB) trust, and explains how to decide which one you need.
- *Plan Your Estate*, by Denis Clifford. This estate planning reference book offers information and advice on all kinds of estate planning strategies,

including lots of material on wills and different kinds of probate-avoidance and tax-saving trusts.

Choosing a Successor Trustee

In your trust document, you must name someone to distribute your trust property to your beneficiaries after your death and to manage it before then if you become incapacitated. The legal term for this person is your successor trustee. (This jargon may be easier to remember if you keep in mind that you're the original trustee—this person is your successor.) To avoid conflicts, it's a good idea to name the same person to be both successor trustee and executor of your will.

Many people choose a grown son or daughter, another relative, or a close friend to serve as successor trustee. It's perfectly legal to name a trust beneficiary—that is, someone who will receive trust property after your death. In fact, it's common.

> **EXAMPLE:** Mildred names her only child, Allison, as both sole beneficiary of her living trust and successor trustee of the living trust. When Mildred dies, Allison uses her authority as trustee to transfer the trust property to herself.

You should choose someone with good judgment, whose integrity you trust completely—and who is likely to outlive you. If you can't come up with anyone who fits this description, think twice about establishing a living trust.

Most people, however, won't have trouble picking a dependable, honest person. Great financial expertise is not usually necessary, because the successor trustee's job is to distribute your assets, not to manage property or investments over the long term (unless you become incapacitated and the trustee takes over before your death). A successor trustee who needs help from an accountant, a lawyer, or a tax preparer usually has authority, under the terms of the trust document, to pay for that help out of trust assets.

In most cases, it makes sense to name just one person as successor trustee, to avoid any possibility of conflicts that could hold up the distribution of trust property to your beneficiaries. But it's legal and may even be desirable to name more than one person. For example, you might name two or more of your children, if you don't expect any disagreements between them and fear that leaving one out would cause hurt feelings. You can also name an alternate successor trustee, in case your first choice isn't available when needed.

The successor trustee does not have to live in the same state as you do, though someone close by will probably have an easier job, especially with real estate transfers. But for transfers of property such as securities and bank accounts, it usually won't make much difference where the successor trustee lives.

Institutions as Successor Trustees

Institutional trustees charge hefty fees, which come out of the trust property and thus leave less for your family and friends. And most aren't interested in "small" trusts—ones that contain less than several hundred thousand dollars worth of property.

But if there's no close relative or friend you can appoint, consider naming a private trust company as successor trustee or as cotrustee with a person. As a rule they charge less than a bank, and your affairs will probably receive more personal attention.

TIP

Don't forget to ask. Before you finalize your living trust, check with the person you've chosen to be your successor trustee, and make sure your choice understands his or her responsibilities and is willing to serve.

Typically, the successor trustee of a simple probate-avoidance living trust isn't paid. This is because in most cases, the successor trustee's only job is to distribute the trust property to beneficiaries soon after the grantor's death. Often, the successor trustee inherits most of the trust property anyway.

An exception is a successor trustee who manages property that stays in trust for a child. In that case, the trust document commonly entitles the successor trustee to "reasonable compensation." The successor trustee decides what is reasonable and takes it from the trust property left to the young beneficiary.

> **RESOURCE**
> *The Trustee's Legal Companion*, **by Liza Hanks and Carol Elias Zolla (Nolo), is a great guide for anyone serving as a successor trustee.** It explains where to start, what the trustee's responsibilities are, and how to get help from lawyers and other experts.

Leaving Trust Property to Young Beneficiaries

If any of your beneficiaries might inherit trust property before they're legally adults (18, in most states), you should definitely arrange for an adult to manage the property on their behalf. Minors are not allowed to control significant amounts of property, and if you haven't provided someone to do it, a court may have to appoint a property guardian. You can, if you wish, also arrange for management for older beneficiaries who are adults in the eyes of the law, but not necessarily in yours.

There are two main ways to accomplish this goal:

- Leave the property in trust, to be managed by the successor trustee, or
- Name a custodian to manage the property.

Leaving the property in trust. In the trust document, you can state that if a beneficiary is under a certain age at your death, the property he or she is to inherit stays in trust. To distinguish it, the child's trust is often called a "subtrust" of the original living trust.

The successor trustee (or your spouse, if you created a shared trust) manages the property until the beneficiary reaches the age you designated.

> **EXAMPLE:** Roger leaves living trust property to his grandson, Alex, with the stipulation that if Alex is not yet 25 when Roger dies, the property will stay in trust to be used for his benefit. At Roger's death, Alex is just 17. The successor trustee of Roger's trust is his daughter Julia, who is Alex's mother. She takes control of the property, spending money on Alex's education and other allowed expenses, until his 25th birthday. Then he gets whatever is left.

Naming a custodian. Instead of keeping the child's property in a trust, you may want instead to appoint a "custodian" to manage it. This option is available in all but a few states, under a law called the Uniform Transfers to Minors Act. (It's discussed fully in Chapter 1.)

The custodian you choose manages the property until the child reaches an age specified by your state's law: 21 in most states, but up to 25 in a few. Like a trustee, the custodian has a legal duty to act honestly and responsibly—but is not supervised by any court.

Dealing with banks and other institutions may also be easier for the custodian than for a trustee, because banks are familiar with the custodian's legal authority, which is determined by state law. A trustee's powers, on the other hand, come only from the trust document. Because every trust document is unique, a bank may want to examine yours and submit it for a review by bank lawyers, to make sure of the trustee's authority.

Because a custodianship must end at the age your state law dictates, it's not as flexible as a trust. But it works just fine if you don't leave a huge amount to the child and suspect that most of it will be spent by the time the child turns 21.

Sample Living Trust Document (Page 1)

Declaration of Trust

Part 1. Trust Name
This revocable living trust shall be known as The Judith M. Avery Revocable Living Trust.

Part 2. Declaration of Trust
Judith M. Avery, called the grantor, declares that she has transferred and delivered to the trustee all her interest in the property described in Schedule A attached to this Declaration of Trust. All of that property is called the "trust property." The trustee hereby acknowledges receipt of the trust property and agrees to hold the trust property in trust, according to this Declaration of Trust.

The grantor may add property to the trust.

Part 3. Terminology
The term "this Declaration of Trust" includes any provisions added by valid amendment.

Part 4. Amendment and Revocation

A. Amendment or Revocation by Grantor
The grantor may amend or revoke this trust at any time, without notifying any beneficiary. An amendment must be made in writing and signed by the grantor. Revocation may be in writing or any manner allowed by law.

B. Amendment or Revocation by Other Person
The power to revoke or amend this trust is personal to the grantor. A conservator, guardian, or other person shall not exercise it on behalf of the grantor, unless the grantor specifically grants a power to revoke or amend this trust in a Durable Power of Attorney.

Part 5. Payments From Trust During Grantor's Lifetime
The trustee shall pay to or use for the benefit of the grantor as much of the net income and principal of the trust property as the grantor requests. Income shall be paid to the grantor at least annually.

Part 6. Trustees

A. Trustee
Judith M. Avery shall be trustee of this trust.

B. Trustee's Responsibility
The trustee in office shall serve as trustee of all trusts created under this Declaration of Trust, including children's subtrusts.

Transferring Property to the Trust

Once you have a signed, notarized trust document, there is one more essential step to making your living trust effective. You must make sure that ownership of all the property you listed in the trust document is legally transferred to yourself as trustee of the living trust.

When living trusts fail, it is usually because the property listed in the trust document was not actually transferred to the trust. If property isn't properly transferred, the terms of the Declaration of Trust have no effect on it. At your death, it will pass under the terms of your will. If there is no will, it will go to your closest relatives under your state's "intestate succession" law.

Items with title documents. To transfer real estate, stocks, mutual funds, bonds, money market accounts, vehicles, or other property with title documents, you must change the title document to show that you own the property in your capacity as trustee. For example, if you want to put your house into your living trust, you must prepare and sign a new deed, transferring ownership from you to yourself as trustee.

Items without title documents. If an item of property doesn't have a title (ownership) document, listing it in the trust document is generally enough to transfer it. So, for example, no additional paperwork is required for most books, furniture, electronics, jewelry, appliances, musical instruments, and many other kinds of property. If, however, an item is particularly valuable, you may want to prepare a simple document that states you are officially transferring ownership to yourself as trustee. And if you're making a trust in New York, state law requires you to prepare a separate transfer document for all property.

What Property to Put in a Trust

You're creating a revocable living trust primarily to avoid probate fees. So here's the key rule to keep in mind: Generally, the more an item is worth, the more it will cost to probate it. That means if you create a trust, you should transfer at least your most valuable property items to it. Think about including:

- houses and other real estate
- stock, bond, and other security accounts held by brokerages (if you can't or don't want to name a TOD beneficiary, as described in Chapter 3)
- small business interests (stock in a closely held corporation, partnership interests, or limited liability company shares)
- patents and copyrights
- precious metals
- jewelry, antiques, furs, and valuable furniture
- valuable works of art, and
- valuable collections of stamps, coins, or other objects.

Adding Property Later

You can add property to your living trust at any time. And as trustee, you can always sell or give away property in the trust. You can also take it out of the living trust and put it back in your name as an individual.

You don't need to put everything you own into a living trust to save money on probate. For some assets, you may decide to use other probate-avoidance devices instead. (Some options are described below; also, check the table in the Introduction for a thorough list of alternatives for different kinds of property.)

Even if some nontrust property does have to go through regular probate, attorney and appraisal fees generally correspond roughly to the value of the probated property, so they'll be relatively low.

Real Estate

If you're like most people, the most valuable thing you own is real estate: your house, condominium, or land. Many people create a living trust just to make sure a house doesn't go through probate. You can probably save your family substantial probate costs by transferring your real estate through a living trust.

Co-op apartments. If you own shares in a co-op corporation and want to transfer them to your living trust, you may run into difficulties with the corporation. Some (although this is fast changing) are reluctant to let a trustee—even though the trust is completely controlled by the grantor—own shares. Check the co-op corporation's rules to see if the transfer is allowed.

CAUTION

Look out for transfer taxes. In most states, transfers of real estate to revocable living trusts are exempt from transfer taxes usually imposed on real estate sales. But check with local property tax officials to make sure that transferring real estate to your living trust won't trigger a tax.

CAUTION

Check with the title company before you change title. A title company could take the position that holding real estate in trust cancels your title insurance policy. If this is a concern, check first.

TIP

Don't overlook simpler alternatives. If you already co-own real estate with someone else, you may not need a living trust right now. (See Chapter 6.) And in some states, you can prepare a deed now but have it take effect only at your death. These "transfer-on-death" deeds are discussed in Chapter 5.

Small Business Interests

Tying up an ongoing small business during probate can be disastrous. Not only does your executor have to run the business for many months, but a court must supervise. Using a living trust to transfer business interests to beneficiaries quickly after your death is almost essential if you want them to take over the business and keep it running.

Different kinds of business organizations present different issues when you want to transfer your interest to your living trust:

Sole proprietorships. If you (or you and your spouse) operate your business as a sole proprietorship, with all business assets held in your own name, you can simply transfer your business property to your living trust as you would any other property. You should also transfer the business's name itself: That transfers the customer goodwill associated with the name.

Partnership interests. If you operate your business with partners, you should be able to easily transfer your partnership share to your living trust. If there is a partnership ownership certificate, it must be changed to include the trust as owner of your share.

It's not common, but a partnership agreement may limit or forbid transfers to a living trust. If yours does, you and your partners may want to see a lawyer before you make any changes.

Closely held corporations. A closely held corporation is a corporation that is not authorized to sell shares to the public. All its shares are owned by a few people (or just one) who are actively involved in running the business (or are relatives of people who are). Normally, you can use a living trust to transfer shares in a closely held corporation by listing the stock in the trust document and then having the stock certificates reissued in your name as trustee.

You'll want to check the corporation's bylaws and any shareholders' agreements, in case there are restrictions on your freedom to transfer your shares to a living trust. Also make sure that if you hold the shares in trust, you will still have voting rights in your capacity as trustee of the living trust; usually, this is not a problem. If it is, you and the other shareholders should be able to amend the corporation's bylaws to allow it.

One fairly common rule is that surviving shareholders (or the corporation itself) have the right to buy the shares of a deceased shareholder. In that case, you can still use a living trust to transfer the shares, but the people who inherit them may have to sell them to the other shareholders.

Limited liability companies. If your small business is an LLC, you'll need the consent of a majority or all of the other owners (check your operating agreement) before you can transfer your interest to your living trust. Getting the other owners to agree shouldn't be a problem; they'll just want to know that you, as trustee of your own trust, will have authority to vote on LLC decisions. You may also want to modify your trust document to give the trustee (that's you) specific authority to participate in the limited liability company. Another way to address this concern would be to transfer your economic interest in the LLC, but not your right to vote. The transfer itself isn't hard—you can prepare your own form and call it an assignment of interest.

Bank Accounts

It's not difficult to hold bank accounts in your living trust. You just need to change the paperwork held by the bank, savings and loan, or credit union.

It's sometimes inconvenient, however, to have bank accounts owned in the name of a trust. That's especially true for personal checking accounts—it's not always easy to write a check at a convenience store at 10 p.m. if the account is owned by a revocable living trust.

> **TIP**
> **Consider the alternatives.** Instead of using a living trust, consider adding a payable-on-death beneficiary to your account. At your death, what's left in those accounts will go directly to the beneficiary, without probate. (See Chapter 1.)

Individual Retirement Accounts

Individual retirement accounts can't be assigned to a trust; you, as an individual, must own your accounts. You can, however, name a trust as a beneficiary. (See Chapter 2.)

Vehicles

Some kinds of property are cumbersome to keep in a living trust. It's not a legal problem, just a practical one. Cars or other vehicles you use regularly are a good example. Having registration and insurance in the trustee's name could be confusing, and some lenders and insurance companies are flummoxed by cars that technically are owned by living trusts.

If you have valuable antique autos, or a mobile home that is permanently attached to land and considered real estate under your state's law, however, you may want to go ahead and transfer ownership to your living trust. You should be able to find an insurance company that will cooperate.

TIP
Check out special transfer procedures for vehicles. Chapter 4 discusses several ways, simpler than a living trust, to avoid probate for vehicles.

Property You Buy or Sell Frequently

If you don't expect to own an item of property at your death, there's no compelling reason to transfer it to your living trust. Remember, the probate process you want to avoid doesn't happen until after your death. On the other hand, if you're buying property, it's usually not much more trouble to acquire and own it in the name of the trust.

Stocks and bonds. Even if you buy and sell securities regularly, there's no problem with having them in a living trust. See "Securities," below.

Life Insurance

If you own a life insurance policy at your death, the proceeds that the named beneficiary receives do not go through probate. (They are, however, considered part of your estate for federal estate tax purposes.)

If a child is the beneficiary of your policy, however, you may want to take an additional step to make sure someone will manage the money for the child if necessary. It's not difficult; you just name your living trust as the beneficiary. Then, in the trust document, specify that the proceeds should be managed by an adult if the child is still young when you die. If you don't arrange for management of the money, and the child receives the money while still a minor, a court will have to appoint a financial guardian to handle the money.

Securities

It's easy for you to register stocks, bonds, and mutual funds as trustee of your living trust; all brokers and mutual fund companies will help you. It's even easier if you set up accounts to consolidate all your investments at a big investment company, such as Charles Schwab, Vanguard, or Fidelity. You can put your whole account into the living trust, and then automatically buy and sell securities in the name of the trustee.

Once the account is in the trustee's name, all securities in the account are then held in trust. That means you can use your living trust to leave all the contents of the account to a specific beneficiary. If you want to leave stock to different beneficiaries, you can either establish more than one brokerage account or leave the contents of a single account to more than one beneficiary to own together.

Stock in closely held corporations. See "Small Business Interests," above.

> **TIP**
>
> **Consider transfer-on-death registration instead.** Almost all states now allow ownership of securities to be registered in "transfer-on-death" form. In those states, you can designate someone to receive your securities, including mutual funds and brokerage accounts, after your death. No probate will be necessary. (See Chapter 3.)

Cash

It's common for people to want to leave cash to beneficiaries—for example, to leave $5,000 to a relative, friend, or charity. There's no way, however, to transfer cash to a living trust.

You can, however, easily accomplish the same goal by transferring ownership of a cash account—savings account, money market account, or certificate of deposit, for example—to your living trust. You can then name a beneficiary to receive the contents of the account. So if you want to leave $5,000 to cousin Fred, all you have to do is put the money in a bank or money market account, transfer it to yourself as trustee, and name Fred in the trust document as the beneficiary.

If you don't want to set up a separate account to leave a modest amount of cash to a beneficiary, think about buying a savings bond and designating a payable-on-death beneficiary, or leaving one larger account, through your trust, to several beneficiaries.

Taxes and Record Keeping

After a revocable living trust is created, little day-to-day record keeping is required.

Whenever you transfer property to or from the trust, however, it must be done in writing. That isn't difficult unless you transfer a lot of property in and out of the trust.

> EXAMPLE: Monica and David Fielding put their house in a living trust to avoid probate, but later decide to sell it. In the real estate contract and deed transferring ownership to the new owners, Monica and David sign their names "as trustees of the Monica and David Fielding Revocable Living Trust."

> ### Registering the Trust
>
> Some states (Alaska, Hawaii, Idaho, Michigan, Missouri, and Nebraska) require that you register your living trust document with the local court. But there are no legal consequences or penalties if you don't. Registration entails filing some basic information about the trust—not all its terms—with the court.

No separate income tax records or returns are necessary as long as you are both the grantor and the trustee. (IRS Reg. § 1.671-4.) Income from property in the living trust must be reported on your personal income tax return; you don't have to file a separate tax return for the trust.

Amending or Revoking a Living Trust Document

One of the most attractive features of a revocable living trust is its flexibility: You can change its terms, or end it altogether, at any time.

If you created a shared trust with your spouse, either of you can revoke it. If, however, you want to change any trust provisions—for example, change a beneficiary or successor trustee—both of you must agree in writing. And both spouses will probably have to consent to transfer real estate out of the living trust; buyers and title insurance companies usually insist on both spouses' signatures on transfer documents. After one spouse dies, the surviving spouse is free to amend the terms of the trust document that deal with his or her property, but can't change the parts that determine what happens to the deceased spouse's trust property.

Amending or Revoking Your Living Trust

You may need to amend if...	You may need to revoke if...
• You get married.	• You want to make extensive, possibly confusing revisions.
• You have a child.	• You get divorced.
• You add valuable property to the trust.	
• You change your mind about whom you want to inherit certain items of trust property or whom you want to serve as successor trustee.	
• You move to a state with different laws about marital property or property management for young beneficiaries.	
• Your spouse dies.	
• A major beneficiary dies.	

Take Advantage of Special Procedures for Small Estates

Why Even Large Estates May Qualify 157

    What Kinds of Property Count 157

    Subtracting What You Owe on Property 159

    If There's No Dollar Limit 159

    Using These Rules to Plan 160

Claiming Wages With an Affidavit 160

Claiming Other Property With Affidavits 162

Simplified Court Procedures 166

    An Overview 166

    Is a Lawyer Necessary? 168

    State Rules 168

Probate has a deservedly bad name, and the best solution would be to do away with it for uncontested cases—but that isn't going to happen any time soon. States have begun, however, to let some people slip out of the probate requirement.

Who gets out? As you might guess, one big category comprises people who don't leave much of monetary value—and whose probate cases aren't worth much to lawyers. "Small estates are a plague to the courts and lawyers as well as the debtors," wrote one official commentator dismissively. (Comments to Ind. Stat. Ann. § 29-1-8-1.)

Because of the way the laws are written, however, not only small estates can benefit. Many estates worth hundreds of thousands of dollars legally qualify as "small estates," eligible for special transfer procedures that speed property to inheritors.

There are two basic kinds of probate shortcuts for small estates:

- **Claiming property with affidavits—no court required.** If the total value of all the assets you leave behind is less than a certain amount, the people who inherit your personal property—that's anything except real estate—may be able to skip probate entirely. The exact amount depends on state law, and varies hugely. Wyoming's limit, $200,000, is the highest. If the estate qualifies, an inheritor can prepare a short document stating that he or she is entitled to a certain item of property under a will or state law. This paper, signed under oath, is called an affidavit. When the person or institution holding the property—for example, a bank where the deceased person had an account—receives the affidavit and a copy of the death certificate, it releases the money or other property.

- **Simplified court procedures.** Another option for small estates (again, as defined by state law) is a quicker, simpler version of probate. The probate court is still involved, but it exerts far less control over the settling of the estate. In many states, these procedures are straightforward enough to handle without a lawyer, so they save money as well as time.

Most states have both kinds of procedures; some have just one. A complete state-by-state listing is in the appendix.

Why Even Large Estates May Qualify

If you're sure that you will leave behind assets worth much more than your state's dollar limit, you probably assume that the simple procedures described in this chapter won't be available to your inheritors. Not so fast. Even if the value of your estate is bigger—much bigger—than your state's limit, your inheritors may still be able to take advantage of the simpler procedures.

The reason is that in adding up the value of your estate to see if it is under the dollar limit, many states exclude huge chunks of assets. It's conceivable that in some states, a $500,000 estate could qualify for "small estate" procedures.

If you plan ahead and learn about your state's rules (keeping in mind, of course, that they may change before your death), chances are good that you can adjust your affairs so that you will leave a "small estate" as your state defines it.

You can find summaries of each state's rules in the appendix. The rest of this section tells you what to look for and how to make sense of what you find.

What Kinds of Property Count

Many states simply don't consider the value of certain kinds of valuable property—for example, motor vehicles, real estate, or real estate located in another state. And possibly more important, many states don't count the value of property that won't go through probate. That means your probate-avoidance work pays double dividends after your death. Making sure your bank accounts and real estate won't go through probate, for example, not only saves on those probate costs but might also enable other property to escape probate, too.

EXAMPLE 1: Robert, a California resident, dies owning a car worth $18,000 and a half-interest in the following assets, worth almost $400,000:

- an IRA worth $150,000
- a payable-on-death bank account with $10,000 in it
- $20,000 worth of stocks, and
- a house worth $400,000, which he owns as community property with right of survivorship with his wife.

The limit for "small estates" in California is $150,000, but vehicles, payable-on-death accounts, and property that goes to a surviving spouse aren't counted toward that limit. So only the stocks count toward the $150,000 limit, allowing Robert's estate to qualify for small estate procedures.

EXAMPLE 2: Tina lives in Indiana, which restricts use of its affidavit procedure to estates worth no more than $50,000. That won't help me, thinks Tina, who expects to leave more than $200,000 worth of property at her death. But she's wrong. When it comes to this limit, Indiana, like a fair number of other states, only counts assets that would otherwise go through probate.

Here's how Tina's estate breaks down:

- her house, worth $100,000, which she has transferred to a living trust to avoid probate
- securities, worth $40,000, that she has registered in beneficiary (TOD) form
- checking and savings bank accounts containing $30,000
- a $40,000 retirement account for which she's named a beneficiary, and
- miscellaneous personal property and household items worth $10,000.

Because only the bank accounts and the $10,000 of miscellaneous items are subject to probate, Tina has a "small estate" under Indiana law. Her inheritors will be able to use the affidavit procedure to claim the household items, and no probate will be necessary.

Subtracting What You Owe on Property

When you're trying to figure out whether or not your estate will be small enough to escape probate, some states require you to use the market value of your property; others instruct you to subtract any amounts owed on it. It can make a huge difference, of course.

> EXAMPLE: Millie, a childless widow, dies owning personal property—a car, some stocks, bank accounts, and household furnishings—with a total market value of $45,000. Missouri law says that her inheritors can claim the property without probate if the total value, less "liens and encumbrances," is no greater than $40,000. Because Millie still owed $7,000 on her car when she died, that amount (a lien on the car) can be subtracted. That brings the total value of her estate to $38,000—low enough to qualify for the small estate procedure.

If There's No Dollar Limit

When it comes to determining who can use simplified probate, a fair number of states don't specify a dollar amount as an upper limit. Instead, they grant small estate status to estates that will be used up by paying certain high-priority debts: the family allowance mandated by law, reasonable funeral and burial expenses, and medical costs of the last illness. The reasoning is that if there's nothing left for other creditors, there's no need for a probate court proceeding. Obviously, estates of very different size will qualify, depending on the debts of the deceased persons.

Using These Rules to Plan

Your state's definition of a small estate is the final piece in the entire probate-avoidance puzzle. Once you understand it, you'll know how much effort you need to devote to other probate-avoidance methods.

For example, say you discover that your state allows up to $70,000 to be transferred by affidavit, and only property that is subject to probate counts toward that limit. You'll know that as long as your most valuable items avoid probate, your executor will be able to use the small estate procedures for a big pile of miscellaneous assets that you have left through your will.

> **TIP**
> **Educate your executor.** Even if your estate qualifies for a simplified probate procedure, it won't do you any good unless your executor knows that the option is available. Too many confused or intimidated executors simply turn everything over to a lawyer, and pay the price.

Claiming Wages With an Affidavit

Most states allow a surviving spouse or other family member to immediately collect, without involving the probate court, salary or wages that were earned by the deceased person. There may be a cap of a few hundred or thousand dollars on the amount that can be collected this way.

Commonly, all the family member needs to do is submit a short statement, signed in front of a notary public, to the employer. It's even simpler than preparing an affidavit under the general procedure, and there's no waiting period. A sample affidavit is shown below.

Sample Affidavit for Collecting Wages

**Affidavit for Collection of Compensation
Owed Deceased Spouse**

I, the undersigned, state as follows:

1. Harold T. Ericson, the decedent, died on July 16, 20xx, at Charleston, West Virginia.
2. I am the surviving spouse of the decedent.
3. No proceeding for the administration of the decedent's estate is pending or has been conducted in any jurisdiction.
4. West Virginia Code § 21-5-8a requires that earnings of the decedent, including compensation for unused vacation, up to $800, be paid promptly to the surviving spouse.
5. I request that I be paid any compensation owed by you for personal services of the decedent, including compensation for unused vacation, not to exceed $800.
6. I declare under penalty of perjury of the laws of West Virginia that the foregoing is true and correct.

_____   _____
Sarah M. Ericson   Date

[Notarization]

Most large employers are familiar with this kind of form; smaller ones, which might have paid the surviving spouse the money even without a formal request, will probably be reassured by it.

Claiming Other Property With Affidavits

An affidavit procedure, happily, dispenses with probate court altogether. If everything in your estate qualifies for this procedure, a probate court will never need to get involved after your death. Instead, inheritors prepare and sign a brief affidavit (sworn statement) saying that they are entitled to use the procedure and to inherit a particular item of property. (There's a sample affidavit, so you can see what one looks like, later in this section.) Then, to get actual possession of the asset, they simply present the affidavit to the person or institution, such as a bank or broker, holding the asset.

There are severe restrictions, however, on who can use this method:

- The property left by the deceased person must be worth less than the ceiling set by state law. These limits vary widely. (Some kinds of property, however, may not count toward the limit, as discussed above.)

- In most states, the procedure can't be used to transfer real estate. A handful of states, however, do provide a special affidavit procedure for real estate. But because real estate transfers are always a matter of public record, the affidavit must be filed in court or with a public agency.

- In most states, inheritors cannot use the affidavit procedure if regular probate court proceedings have begun.

Inheritors can use an affidavit to collect their property whether or not there was a will. In the affidavit, they usually state whether they are inheriting under the terms of a will or under state law. If there's no valid will, your state's "intestate succession" law determines who inherits property. The intestate succession formula is slightly different from state to state, but generally if there are a surviving spouse and children, they inherit everything. If not, then parents, grandchildren, or siblings are next in line.

Affidavit Procedure at a Glance	
Pros	**Cons**
• Doesn't require any action on your part except making sure your executor knows the procedure may be available. • Simple for inheritors to do, and costs nothing.	• Dollar limits restrict procedure to small estates as defined by your state's law. • Can't be used for real estate, except in a few states. • There is a waiting period after death; property can't be transferred to beneficiaries for a month or two. • Not available in all states.

The process of transferring your property to its new owners will be initiated by the people who are inheriting it. Usually, there is a short waiting period—commonly, 30 or 45 days after the death—before anyone is allowed to collect the property.

To get the property, they will present their affidavits and a copy of the death certificate to the person or institution who has possession of the property. Some institutions may also insist on seeing a copy of the will, if any. If the affidavit appears truthful, that person or institution is allowed, by law, to turn over the property without investigating the truth of the statements in the affidavit.

> EXAMPLE: In his will, Perry leaves $20,000 to Alice. A month after Perry dies, Alice goes to his bank and fills out the affidavit form she picks up there, swearing that she is entitled to the money and that the estate qualifies for the state's small estate affidavit procedure. The bank, after looking at the affidavit, a copy of Perry's death certificate, and possibly the will, transfers $20,000 from Perry's account to her.

Banks, other financial institutions, and state motor vehicles agencies, which deal with this sort of transfer all the time, may have their own affidavit forms for people to fill out. Otherwise, the claimants may have to put together their own, making sure it covers all the conditions the state statute requires. Generally, an affidavit must include statements to the effect that:

- The value of the probate estate does not exceed the statutory limit.
- The required waiting period has elapsed since the death.
- No probate court proceedings have been initiated.
- The claimant is entitled to the property. Although it's not always required by statute, it's a good idea for the claimant to explain the basis of the claim—for example, because of the deceased person's will or state intestate succession law.

The affidavit may need to be notarized—that is, signed in front of a notary public—or it may be enough for it to include a statement to the effect that it is being signed "under penalty of perjury."

A sample affidavit, from Minnesota, is shown below.

In most states, an affidavit needs to be given only to the entity that is holding the property. But some states now require a copy to be sent to the state taxing agency, in case any state taxes are due. If the deceased person received any public benefits, another copy may need to go to the health or welfare department; if there's money left in the estate, the government will want to be reimbursed for the aid it provided.

Most banks, brokers, and other entities your inheritors will likely deal with are quite familiar with the affidavit process. But if one refuses to cooperate, just showing an unhelpful clerk a copy of the statute (readily available online or at a public law library) should melt away the opposition. If that doesn't get results, chances are a phone call or letter from a local lawyer will. And as a last resort, the inheritor can go to court—small claims court, if possible—and demand that the assets be turned over.

Sample Affidavit

Affidavit for Collection of Personal Property
Under Minnesota Statutes 524.3-1201

I, the undersigned, state as follows:

1. _____ , the decedent,

   died on _____ .

2. The value of the entire probate estate, determined as of the date of death, wherever located, including specifically any contents of a safe deposit box, less liens and encumbrances, does not exceed $20,000.

3. At least thirty days have elapsed since the decedent's death, as shown by the attached certified copy of the decedent's death certificate.

4. No application or petition for the appointment of a personal representative is pending or has been granted in any jurisdiction.

5. I, the undersigned, am entitled to payment or delivery, under the terms of the decedent's will, of the following property:

6. I declare that the foregoing is true and correct.

_____   _____

Signature   Date

[Notarization]

RESOURCE

Help for California readers. For a California affidavit form and instructions on how to use it, see *How to Probate an Estate in California*, by Julia Nissley (Nolo).

Simplified Court Procedures

Even if your estate doesn't qualify for the affidavit procedure, or not all your property can be transferred that way, there may still be hope for avoiding a full-fledged probate proceeding. Nearly all states offer something called "summary probate" or "informal probate," which is more complex than the out-of-court affidavit procedure but not nearly as bothersome as regular probate.

Simplified Probate at a Glance	
Pros	**Cons**
• Doesn't require any action on your part except making sure your executor knows the procedure may be available. • A good fallback for property you don't specifically use a probate-avoidance method for.	• Dollar limits restrict procedure to small estates as defined by your state's law. • In some states, limited to surviving spouse or children. • There is a waiting period after death; property can't be transferred to beneficiaries for a month or two. • Your executor may need to hire a lawyer. • Not available in all states.

An Overview

A summary probate is started by the person named in the will to serve as executor (also called personal representative) of the estate. (If there's no will, the surviving spouse, or another relative who stands to inherit, usually takes the initiative.) That person—let's call him or her the executor, which is what most courts do—files a document (commonly called a petition or an affidavit) with the local probate court, requesting the simpler process. Most states impose a waiting period of a month or two before the petition may be filed. Specific requirements vary from state to state, but in most cases the petition must:

- say that the estate qualifies as a "small estate," as state law defines that term
- list the persons or organizations entitled to inherit the property
- state that no request for formal probate has been made, and
- state that all (or certain) debts and taxes have been paid.

The executor will probably also need to submit a copy of the death certificate, the deceased person's will, if there is one, and an inventory and appraisal of all the deceased person's assets.

If everything is in order, the probate court will authorize the summary procedure, and basically that's the end of court supervision. The executor may be required to notify creditors and people who might inherit (under the will or state law) of the death and the probate proceedings, or to publish a notice in a local newspaper. Many states, however, don't require this. Otherwise, the bills can be paid and the assets distributed immediately, without further ado. Generally, the executor is also required to file a closing statement with the court, showing where everything went.

TIP

Use simplified probate as interim estate planning. Conducting a simplified probate procedure, while an improvement over regular probate, still isn't nearly as easy as winding up a living trust or using the other probate-avoidance methods in this book. For most people, it's best to think of simplified probate as a fallback method of avoiding probate; if you're young and healthy, you may decide to put off creating a trust until later in life, knowing that, if necessary, simplified probate procedures will ease things for your loved ones.

Is a Lawyer Necessary?

Even a new-and-improved simple probate may still require a fair amount of paperwork. Everything can, however, probably be done by mail; no court appearances should be necessary.

How easy it will be for someone to tackle a summary probate depends to a large extent on whether or not good do-it-yourself materials are available and on how helpful the probate court is. Some courts provide good explanatory materials and forms, and court clerks help people along. Others, unfortunately, expect people to figure out every detail themselves.

If that's the situation where you live, someone who goes this route after your death may want to get advice from an experienced lawyer or paralegal. That doesn't mean turning the whole process over to a professional—but having someone available to help smooth over any rough patches can make a huge difference.

Even if a lawyer is consulted, the overall cost of simplified probate should be less than that of regular probate. The process will be over more quickly, too.

RESOURCE

Help for California readers. For complete instructions on handling a summary probate without a lawyer in California, see *How to Probate an Estate in California*, by Julia Nissley (Nolo).

State Rules

Brief descriptions of who qualifies for each state's simplified probate procedures are in the appendix.

Each state's actual court procedure, however, is different. If you're interested in the details—what kind of documents are currently required and how long the process takes—you'll have to ask someone at your local court or read your state's statutes themselves.

You can find a statute online or at a large public library or county law library, by looking up its citation (listed after each description): If you're looking online, start at www.nolo.com and follow the links to your state's statutes. If you go to a library, a law librarian can quickly help you get to the right book. Keep in mind, though, that these statutes change; years from now, the rules and procedures may be very different.

Make Gifts

The Federal Gift Tax..173

Making Tax-Free Gifts..174

    Gifts of Up to the Annual Exclusion Amount 174

    Gifts for Tuition or Medical Bills 176

    Gifts to Your Spouse.. 177

    Gifts to Charities 178

Gifts That Could Land You in Tax Trouble..179

    Loans That Are Really Gifts 179

    Gifts Made to One Person but Intended for Another 180

    Gifts With Strings Attached 181

What to Give..181

    Property That Is Likely to Increase in Value....................................... 182

    Property That Has Increased in Value... 182

Gifts to Children 183

    Who Will Manage the Property?.. 184

    Special Gift Tax Rules 185

    Income Tax Considerations... 186

Thinking Before You Give...186

Giving away property while you're alive is very different from the other probate-avoidance strategies in this book, which all involve leaving things to people at your death. For one, gifts made during life are generous in a way that gifts at death can never be. After all, it's no sacrifice to part with things only when you cannot—beyond a doubt—use them anymore. Making gifts requires you to give up something now. In return, it gives you the joy of watching your gifts help people you love or organizations you admire.

Making gifts helps you avoid probate for a very simple reason: If you don't own something when you die, it doesn't have to go through probate. That lowers probate costs because, as a general rule, the higher the monetary value of the assets that go through probate, the higher the expense. If you give away enough assets, your estate might even qualify for a streamlined "small estate" probate procedure after your death. (See Chapter 8.)

All you need to make a gift is a checkbook; no fancy documents (or legal fees) are required. But before you embark on a gift-giving program, you should understand a little about federal gift tax. Sorry.

Gift Giving at a Glance	
Pros	**Cons**
• It's easy to do. • You get to see your gifts enjoyed by the recipients. • Giving property away saves estate taxes, if your estate will be large enough to be subject to them.	• Once you give property away, it's gone for good. • Large gifts—currently, more than $14,000 per recipient per year—require a federal gift tax return and may be subject to tax. • Gifts to minors are subject to special rules to keep their tax-free status.

The Federal Gift Tax

Making large gifts is usually a tax-saving strategy, not a probate-avoidance one. Wealthy people give away property so that when they die, there will be less property to tax. The tax that the givers are trying to reduce or eliminate is the federal "gift and estate tax."

Estate tax is a concern for very few Americans; fewer than 1% of estates file estate tax returns. Currently, gift or estate tax is an issue only if:

- during your life, you give away more than $5.34 million (2014 amount) in taxable gifts (many kinds of gifts are tax-free, as discussed below), or
- at your death, the value of the taxable property you leave behind (property left to your spouse or a tax-exempt charity isn't taxable) plus taxable gifts you made during life, is more than $5.34 million.

The gift/estate tax exemption amount is indexed for inflation and increases every year.

Why worry about gift and estate taxes at all if you don't ever expect your net worth to cross the estate tax threshold? One reason is that if you make large gifts—currently, more than $14,000 to one recipient in one calendar year—federal law requires you to file a gift tax return, even though you may never owe a penny of tax.

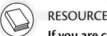 **RESOURCE**

If you are concerned about gift and estate taxes, get more information. You may want to start with the articles on estate tax at www.nolo.com or *Plan Your Estate*, by Denis Clifford, also published by Nolo.

Making Tax-Free Gifts

Many kinds of gifts are exempt from gift tax. If you structure your gifts properly and watch the calendar, you can probably give away as much money as you want without worrying about tax.

All these gifts are exempt from federal gift tax:

- gifts of up to $14,000 per any recipient per year (this amount is indexed for inflation)
- direct payment of someone's tuition or medical bills
- gifts of any amount to your spouse, and
- donations of any amount to tax-exempt charities.

Gifts of Up to the Annual Exclusion Amount

Federal tax law contains a blanket exemption from gift tax for all gifts worth no more than $14,000. (This is the 2014 figure; it is indexed for inflation and will eventually go up.) You can give any number of recipients up to the exempt amount in gifts each calendar year without needing to file a gift tax return. (26 U.S.C. §§ 2503(b), 6019.)

If you're determined to give away lots of money, you can probably stretch this exemption (or exclusion, as the IRS calls it) into a lot more. For example, if you're part of a couple, and are used to thinking of your money together with your mate's, the two of you together have twice the annual exemption per recipient. In fact, even if only one spouse makes a gift, it's considered to have been made by both spouses if they both consent. (26 U.S.C. § 2513.) If you give money to another couple, there's $56,000 tax-free the first year.

> EXAMPLE: Joe and Faye, a couple in their late 70s, want to give their son and his wife money for a down payment on a house. They also see this as an opportunity to get some money out of their estate and reduce the probate and tax bills their son—who will inherit everything anyway—will eventually have to pay.

Both Joe and Faye take advantage of their annual exemption to give a total of $28,000 to their son and another $28,000 to his wife. As soon as the first of the year rolls around, they can give away that much again if they're still feeling well-off and altruistic.

You can make the most of the annual exemption if you keep in mind that it is all based on a calendar year. If you miss a year, you can't go back and claim the exclusion. But if you spread a large gift over two or more years, you may escape gift tax complications.

> **EXAMPLE:** If you give your daughter $20,000 on December 17, $6,000 of that gift is taxable. You'll have to file a gift tax return (by April 15 of the next year) and you'll have used up $6,000 of the total you're allowed to give away or leave tax free.
>
> But if you give her only $10,000 in December, and wait a couple of weeks before handing over the other $10,000 on January 1, both gifts are tax free, and no gift tax return is required.

Not only cash can be split. Give some stocks now, some next year. You can even give real estate in pieces—physical pieces, if that's possible, or pieces of ownership. (For a discussion of what kind of property makes a good gift—from a tax standpoint—see "What to Give," below.)

> **EXAMPLE:** Solomon and his wife Rhoda want to give their vacation cabin to their son Gerard. The cabin is worth $75,000, but their equity is only $40,000; there is still $35,000 left to pay on the mortgage. In November, Solomon and Rhoda sign a deed transferring the house to Rhoda and Gerard as joint tenants. That means that Rhoda and Gerard each own a half-interest in the property. Gerard's share is worth $20,000; the

gift from his parents is tax free because together, they can give him up to $28,000 tax free each calendar year.

The next calendar year, Rhoda gives her half share, worth $20,000 to Gerard. Even though only Rhoda makes the gift, the IRS considers it, for tax purposes, to have come from both spouses.

Ingenious taxpayers (and their lawyers) have come up with all sorts of ways to make the annual exemption work overtime for them. But it's best not to try to get too fancy. Some schemes that may backfire are discussed later in the chapter.

CAUTION
Special rules apply when you make tax-free gifts to children. Gifts to minors must be structured so as not to run afoul of IRS rules. See "Gifts to Children," below.

Gifts for Tuition or Medical Bills

If you pay someone else's tuition or medical bills, the government does not tax your generosity, no matter how great. (26 U.S.C. § 2503(e).)

One very important rule applies: The money must be paid directly to the school or the provider of medical services. If, for example, you write your granddaughter a check for tuition, and she in turn writes a check to the college from her account for exactly the same amount, the gift is not tax free under this provision. It will be tax free, of course, if you give her no more than the annual exclusion amount during the calendar year. (With that in mind, you may want to remind the youngsters in your family of the excellent education available at many public universities.) Similarly, if you reimburse someone who has already paid a medical bill, your gift is not tax free.

Federal law limits what expenses are covered. Here are the rules:

Tuition. Tuition means just that: what a school charges for education or training. You cannot make tax-free gifts for lodging, books, or supplies. The tuition exemption is not, by any means, limited to higher or even academic education. Tuition can be paid to any "educational organization" that has a "regular faculty and curriculum" and a regularly enrolled body of students "in attendance where its educational activities are regularly carried on." (26 U.S.C. §§ 170, 2503(e).) That definition seems to include just about every kind of school except correspondence schools and mail-order diploma mills.

Medical bills. You can pay, gift tax free, for:

- the diagnosis, treatment, or prevention of disease
- transportation primarily for and essential to these kinds of medical care
- insurance (including supplementary medical insurance for the aged) covering these kinds of medical care, or
- lodging of up to $50/night for each individual (as long as it's not "lavish or extravagant under the circumstances," which seems unlikely to be a problem at $50 a night) while away from home, if it's essential to the medical care, if the medical care is provided by a physician in a licensed hospital (or a facility that is related to, or the equivalent of, a licensed hospital), and there is no significant element of personal pleasure in the travel. (26 U.S.C. § 213.)

Cosmetic surgery and similar procedures aren't covered, unless they are necessary because of a disfiguring illness or injury.

Gifts to Your Spouse

All gifts that you make to your spouse are tax free, as long as he or she is a U.S. citizen. If your spouse isn't a citizen, the limit on tax-free gifts is $145,000 in 2014. This amount is indexed for inflation. (26 U.S.C. § 2523(a).)

In practice, there's rarely much of a reason to make large gifts to your spouse. You could actually worsen your tax situation by saddling your spouse with an estate that's so large it will be taxed at his or her death.

Gifts to Charities

If you would like to donate to a charity, the federal government will smile on you. All gifts to tax-exempt charities are exempt from gift tax. (26 U.S.C. § 2522.) If you aren't sure whether or not an organization to which you wish to contribute is tax exempt, just ask a staffer there; someone will be more than happy to help you.

Many people simply write checks to favorite charities. But if you want to make very large gifts and are concerned about gift and estate tax, you may want to consider a different method, involving a charitable gift annuity, donor-advised fund, or charitable trust. In addition to benefiting the charity, it could provide you with income while you're alive and reduce your eventual estate taxes.

Charity Begins With a Trust

There are many varieties of charitable trusts. The most common kind, called a charitable remainder trust, works like this: You set up a trust while you are alive and make an irrevocable gift of property (cash, stocks, or real estate, for example) to it. The charity manages the trust property and distributes a certain part of the income it generates to you or to someone else you've chosen. At your death, the property goes to the charity; because it belonged to the trust, not to you, your estate is not liable for estate tax on it.

For detailed information about different kinds of charitable trusts, see *Plan Your Estate*, by Denis Clifford (Nolo).

Gifts That Could Land You in Tax Trouble

It's the IRS's job to look for estate planning strategies that cross the line from clever to forbidden. Here are a few gift-giving strategies frowned on by the feds. Even if you're not making gifts in order to save on gift and estate tax, you don't want to inadvertently stir up a gift tax problem.

Loans That Are Really Gifts

Some parents have made large loans to their children, intending to forgive the repayments each year, in an amount equal to the annual gift tax exclusion amount. The IRS, skeptical of these arrangements to start with, makes it difficult for families to prove that they are bona fide loans, not gifts in disguise. But the bottom line seems to be that if you are meticulous about your paperwork, this strategy can be successful.

The IRS starts with the presumption that a transfer between family members is a gift. You can get around that presumption by showing that you really expected repayment and intended to enforce the debt. In making that determination, the IRS pays attention to whether or not:

- The borrower signed a promissory note.
- You charged interest.
- There was security (collateral) for the debt.
- You demanded repayment.
- The borrower actually repaid some of the loan.
- There was a fixed date that the loan was due to be repaid.
- The borrower had the ability to repay.
- Your records or those of the recipient indicated that the transfer was a loan.
- The transaction was reported, for federal tax purposes, as a loan.

In the case that prompted this slew of considerations, a woman had loaned $100,000 to each of her two sons. They signed promissory notes, and the loans were duly recorded in the books of the family's business, but there was no deadline for repayment. One of the sons made a $15,000 repayment. Their mother never demanded any payments, and each year she sent a letter to the sons, stating that she had forgiven (canceled) some of the debt. The IRS ruled, and the federal Tax Court agreed, that the loans had actually been gifts. The mother ended up not only owing gift tax on the whole amount, but missing out on the years when she could have been (and thought she was) making tax-free annual gifts. (*Elizabeth B. Miller*, Tax Court Memo 1996-3.)

SEE AN EXPERT

Don't try this yourself. If you want to set up an elaborate scheme for forgiving debts, form is everything. See a lawyer who's experienced in setting up such deals so that they pass IRS scrutiny.

Gifts Made to One Person but Intended for Another

The IRS won't be fooled if you give property to one person but it's obvious that the intended recipient is someone else. For example, the IRS went after the estate of a man who had given annual gifts of stock to his son, daughter-in-law, and grandchildren, classifying each gift as exempt because of the annual gift tax exclusion. For 14 years, the daughter-in-law had faithfully transferred her stock to her husband on the same day she received it. The IRS ruled that the stock was really for the son, and that the gifts to him had exceeded the annual exclusion amount. (*Estate of Joseph Cidulka*, Tax Court Memo 1996-149.)

The gift tax problem doesn't affect the probate-avoidance aspect of the transaction—the stock was out of the man's estate. But shaving a little off your probate costs may be much more trouble than it's worth if it lands you in a skirmish with the IRS.

Gifts With Strings Attached

If you give it, give it. Don't try to hang onto any control over what you've given away, or you'll turn your gift into something else.

> **EXAMPLE:** Carl deeds his house over to his son, Ishmael, but retains the right to receive rent from the property. The transaction is not a legal gift. When Carl dies, the house will still be part of his estate, which means it may be subject to estate tax.

> **TIP**
> **Make a paper trail.** If you think a gift might be questioned later, write up and sign a little statement that explains your intent to make a gift. It will be evidence that you meant to make a gift, if that's ever needed. Such a statement can't turn what is really a loan into a gift, and other evidence may contradict and finally outweigh it—but it can't hurt.

What to Give

Like everything else connected with gift giving, the kind of property you choose to give away—for example, cash, stocks, or real estate— can have tax consequences for you and for the recipient.

> **CAUTION**
> **You can give only what's yours.** If you own property together with your spouse or someone else, you must both consent before you give it away. Especially in community property states (Arizona, California, Idaho, Louisiana, Nevada, New Mexico, Texas, Washington, and Wisconsin), it can

be difficult for married people to know who owns what. See Chapter 6 if you're unsure about community property rules.

Property That Is Likely to Increase in Value

If you're trying to decide what you want to give away, look among your assets for property that you expect to go up in value. If you hold onto it until your death, your estate will be worth that much more, and probate fees (and estate taxes, if your estate is large enough) will be correspondingly higher.

Even if giving away property now is a taxable gift (meaning that some of your personal estate tax exemption will be used up), it may be worth it. Remember that you don't have to actually pay gift and estate tax until you give away or leave more than the exemption amount.

Property That Has Increased in Value

It's usually a poor idea, financially speaking, to give away property that has gone up substantially in value since you acquired it. The reason lies, of course, in the tax code.

When you give someone property, the recipient's tax basis—the amount from which taxable profit or loss is calculated if the property is ever sold—is the same as yours.

> EXAMPLE: Years ago, Vinny paid $100,000 for a piece of land. That amount is his tax basis. Now he gives the land to his niece, Jackie; her tax basis is $100,000, too. If the land is actually worth $150,000 now, and Jackie turns around and sells it, she'll have to pay capital gains tax on her $50,000 gain.

If, on the other hand, you leave property at your death, a different rule applies. The recipient's tax basis is the market value of the property at the date of your death. In short, if the property has increased in value since you bought it, the recipient will get a higher basis—which translates into lower taxes down the line.

> **EXAMPLE:** If Vinny's niece inherits the land from him, her tax basis will be the market value of the property at the time of his death—whether it's more or less than his basis. If the value is still $150,000 when Vinny dies, and Jackie sells the land for that amount, she'll have zero taxable gain.

Obviously, how these rules should affect your actions depends on your particular situation. If you want to make a gift of appreciated property now and expect to live another 25 years, you won't want to postpone the transfer until your death just for some hypothetical income tax savings.

TIP

Different rules apply to charities. There's an important exception to the rule that it's often a bad idea to give away appreciated property: When you're giving to charities, it can be to your financial advantage to donate appreciated property, especially if you're concerned about estate tax. See *Plan Your Estate*, by Denis Clifford (Nolo).

Gifts to Children

Children are the natural objects of their adult relatives' affection and generosity. But giving them valuable property before they are adults in the eyes of the law involves several special considerations.

Who Will Manage the Property?

Minors (in most states, children younger than 18) are not permitted to manage valuable property by themselves; an adult must be responsible. The ceiling varies from state to state, but minors commonly can't own more than a few thousand dollars without adult control.

Fortunately, it's quite easy to choose an adult to manage the property. You can arrange it by setting up either:

- a trust, or
- a custodianship under the Uniform Transfers to Minors Act or the Uniform Gifts to Minors Act.

The easier way is to name an adult to serve as "custodian" of the money. Custodians are authorized under a law called the Uniform Transfers to Minors Act (UTMA) or the Uniform Gifts to Minors Act, one or the other of which has been adopted by every state.

All you need to do is give the property to the adult you choose to be the custodian, instead of to the child directly. The custodian has the legal responsibility to manage and use the money for the benefit of the child. When the child reaches adulthood, the custodian turns over what's left to the beneficiary. In most states, the law requires the property to be turned over to the recipient at 21; in a few states, the age is 18.

> EXAMPLE: Sam wants to give each of his four young grand-children $10,000. He names each child's parent as custodian of the money, and the parents open bank accounts as custodians under the state's Uniform Transfers to Minors Act. They will manage the money until the children turn 21.

State Law Differences

All but two states (South Carolina and Vermont) have adopted the Uniform Transfers to Minors Act, which allows you to name a custodian for property that you give to a minor now or that you leave at your death. The ages at which the custodianships must end in each state are listed in Chapter 1.

The remaining states still have an older law, called the Uniform Gifts to Minors Act, on the books. It authorizes custodians only for gifts made during life, and provides that the custodianship must end when the minor turns 21. The Act also limits the kinds of property that can be given; only money, securities, life insurance policies, and annuity contracts are permitted.

Special Gift Tax Rules

You must be careful if you want to give a tax-free gift to a young beneficiary. It's fine to set up a trust or custodianship (discussed just above) to handle the property for the minor. (Rev. Rul. 59-357, 1959-2.) But to qualify for the annual exclusion, the gift must satisfy these conditions:

- The property and its income may be spent by, or for the benefit of, a recipient who isn't 21 yet. You can give the trustee or custodian authority to decide how much of the income or property should be spent, but you can't limit his or her discretion too strictly.
- The recipient must receive the property outright by age 21. This means that if you create a trust for the recipient, the trust document must state that the property will be turned over to the recipient by his or her 21st birthday. (You may, however, give the recipient the right to extend the trust for a longer period.) Similarly, if you set up a custodianship, it must end

when the recipient turns 21. Some states allow a custodianship to last until the beneficiary is older than 21; don't choose this option if you're concerned about gift tax.

- If the recipient dies before age 21, the remaining property must be payable to the recipient's estate or to someone the recipient named. (26 U.S.C. § 2503(c).)

Income Tax Considerations

Chances are that a minor to whom you make gifts is in a lower income tax bracket than you are. So, if you give income-producing property (stocks, for example) to a minor, he or she will probably pay less tax on the income produced than you would have. But there's an important exception, called the "Kiddie Tax," to this rule. If a gift provides a child younger than 19 (younger than 24, if he or she is a full-time student) with annual income of more than $2,000 (2014 figure), the amount over $2,000 is taxed at his or her parents' highest income tax rate. (26 U.S.C. § 1(g).)

Thinking Before You Give

An ambitious program of gifts is *not* for everyone, especially if your primary financial motivation is probate avoidance, not estate tax savings.

Start with the obvious: When you give something away, it's gone forever. You can't change your mind. For many people, especially as they get older, shedding material things brings a wonderful sense of lightness and freedom. Add to that the pleasure of seeing a younger relative, a friend, or an organization benefit from a gift, and giving can return great satisfaction. But if parting with assets makes you feel vulnerable or nervous, fearful that you will someday be without money you need, don't do it.

These decisions are intensely personal. No formula (or lawyer) can tell you how much wealth you need to be comfortable in your own mind and heart. If you feel torn, it may help you to sit down with pencil and paper (or computer) and make rough estimates of your current assets, future income, and expenses, to get a clearer picture of your actual financial situation.

RESOURCE
Looking ahead. For a sound discussion of how to estimate your retirement income and expenses realistically, see *Retire Happy,* by Ralph Warner and Richard Stim (Nolo).

Putting It All Together

Alice and Frank: A Simple Life 190

Maria: Dealing With Widowhood 192

Mike: Midlife Concerns 196

Jim and Terry: An Unmarried Couple 198

Esther and Mark: New Love, Old Money 201

Linda and Tomas: Comfortable 204

Taken one at a time, the probate-avoidance methods discussed in this book are fairly simple. Still, you may feel a little flummoxed when it's actually time to choose among them and take steps to avoid probate for your assets.

This chapter looks at people in several different life situations and what kinds of probate-avoidance strategies work for them. Of course, everyone's situation is unique; your concerns won't match up perfectly with any of the hypothetical people discussed here. But you'll probably spot enough similarities to get some ideas about where to start.

A reminder: This chapter, like the rest of the book, discusses only planning to avoid probate. It doesn't tackle estate tax, incapacity, or other estate planning issues.

Alice and Frank: A Simple Life

Alice and Frank have always worked hard and have much to show for it: a comfortable home in a small Indiana town, four grown children of whom they are very proud, good friends. What they don't have is a lot of material wealth. Now in their late 60s and retired, they live on Alice's modest company pension, withdrawals from Frank's IRA, and their Social Security payments.

They've always figured that they didn't have enough money to concern themselves with estate planning, especially fancy trusts and the like. They do have straightforward wills, which leave their possessions to each other. The wills name their children as alternate beneficiaries; they'll inherit everything, in equal shares, after both Alice and Frank have died. But Alice and Frank want the kids to inherit their property without needless legal fees, delay, or hassles. That prompts them to look into some simple probate-avoidance techniques.

The house. The couple's most valuable asset is their house. It's long since paid for, and is probably worth about $100,000.

The deed to the property shows that Alice and Frank own it in tenancy by the entirety, a version of joint tenancy limited to married couples. That takes care of probate when the first spouse dies; when that happens, the survivor will own it, without probate. Alice and Frank discuss putting the house in joint tenancy with the children, but decide against it. They love their children, but just don't feel completely comfortable giving away ownership rights in the house.

They decide, finally, to make a simple living trust, and transfer only their house to it. They name all the children as beneficiaries, and their daughter Nancy as successor trustee. They've already named her to be executor of their wills. It will fall to her, as successor trustee, to transfer ownership of the house to all the children after both parents have died.

Bank accounts. Aside from the house, the couple's main asset is a savings account. It's held in joint tenancy with the right of survivorship. That means that when Frank or Alice dies, the survivor will automatically own the entire account, without probate. Alice and Frank could transfer the account to their living trust, but decide it's even easier to make their children payable-on-death (POD) beneficiaries for the account, so that when the survivor dies, any remaining funds will go directly to the children, again without probate.

They go to the bank, where a clerk gives them a short form to fill out. Then they list their children's names as the payable-on-death beneficiaries, sign the form, and give it back to the clerk. While they're at it, they do the same thing with their joint checking account. It doesn't have a lot of money in it, but that's all the more reason, they decide, to make sure it doesn't have to get tangled up in probate. The whole process takes ten minutes and costs nothing.

Frank's IRA. On a form provided by the bank that handles his IRA, Frank has already named Alice as the beneficiary for this account. If he dies first, she'll inherit the money. If she dies before he does, the children are named as alternates. No probate will be necessary.

Alice and Frank decide that this is all the probate-avoidance planning they need. The rest of their property, which they'll leave through their wills, should fall below the $50,000 cutoff for "small estates" under Indiana law. That means that it will qualify for simplified transfer procedures, which shouldn't be expensive or burdensome for the children.

Alice and Frank's Probate-Avoidance Plan	
Asset	**Plan**
House	Change from tenancy by the entirety to a simple living trust.
Bank accounts	Keep in joint tenancy; also name payable-on-death beneficiaries to inherit the funds after both parents have died.
Frank's IRA	No action needed; Frank has already named a beneficiary, on a form provided by the bank that administers his IRA account.
Everything else (car, household belongings)	Leave to each other by will. Should pass under Indiana simplified "small estate" procedures.

Maria: Dealing With Widowhood

Maria is an Illinois widow in her 70s with a son and daughter in their 40s and two grandchildren, her son's children. When her husband died six years ago, she inherited everything he owned. Their house had been held in joint tenancy, and was easy to transfer into her name after his death. Other assets, however, had to go through probate. Maria found the process confusing, tiring, and expensive. She is determined to spare her two children the burden of probate, as much as is reasonably possible, at her death.

To that end, she takes a quick inventory of her property. The most valuable asset is the house, which has risen to $350,000 in value. The mortgage has been paid in full. She also owns two sizable mutual fund accounts, some IBM stock, some certificates of deposit at her bank, and a checking account. Some of Maria's other possessions aren't particularly economically valuable, but they are precious to her: a collection of stamps that she wants her grandson to inherit and the family china that she wants to pass on to her daughter.

Maria's will was written 15 years ago, while her husband was alive and before their grandchildren were born. It leaves her entire estate to him, with their son and daughter as alternate beneficiaries. It would still work to pass her property to her children, but everything would have to go through probate, and it wouldn't leave the china or stamps to the people she now has in mind. Maria decides she would like both to avoid probate and fine-tune the way she leaves her property.

Bank accounts. First, Maria tackles the easy things. The bank accounts and CDs are quickly turned into payable-on-death accounts, with her son and daughter as the POD beneficiaries. The bank provides the form; all Maria has to do is list their names. The bank confirms that all the payees will have to do, to collect the funds after Maria's death, is present a copy of her death certificate, and identification, to the bank.

Stocks and mutual fund accounts. The stock accounts are also simple to handle, although the paperwork takes a bit longer. Because she lives in Illinois, which allows transfer-on-death registration of securities, she can simply reregister her ownership in transfer-on-death (TOD) form. Like the POD bank accounts, stock held this way will pass without probate to the beneficiaries she names.

Maria calls the mutual fund company and explains that she wants to register her ownership in transfer-on-death form. The company sends her a form to fill out, on which she lists her son and daughter as beneficiaries.

Maria also reregisters the IBM stock; her broker contacts the company's transfer agent to get the paperwork. But she wants her son's children, who are both minors, to inherit this stock. So she names as beneficiary her son, as "custodian" for each of the grandchildren, under the Illinois Uniform Transfers to Minors Act. That way if the grandchildren inherit the stock before they turn 21, their father will manage it for them. (The Uniform Transfers to Minors Act is explained in Chapter 1.)

The house. Maria decides that a living trust is the best way to avoid probate for her house. So she creates a trust and signs a new deed, transferring the house to herself as trustee of her living trust. She names her children as the trust beneficiaries. Another option would be an Illinois Transfer on Death Instrument, which would let Maria record a deed, naming her son and daughter as TOD beneficiaries of the house.

Heirlooms. Because she's created a living trust, Maria decides to use it to leave some heirlooms—the stamp collection, set of china, and a few others, so they won't have to go through probate. So in the trust document, she leaves the stamps to her grandson, the china to her daughter, and a few other items to her son.

The car. Maria's car is an old Mercedes that her son has always loved. Maria decides to name her son on the title as the transfer-on-death (TOD) beneficiary. That way, he will inherit it at her death, without probate.

The leftovers. Finally, Maria makes a new will. Because she has taken care of almost everything in her trust, the will is short and simple. It says only that anything not specifically left by another method should go to her son and daughter, in equal shares. The will is essentially a back-up device, so that Maria knows that everything is taken care of. And Illinois's special procedures for small estates allow up to $100,000 of property to avoid regular probate.

Maria's Probate-Avoidance Plan	
Asset	**Plan**
House	Transfer by living trust.
Bank accounts and CDs	Name payable-on-death beneficiaries.
IBM stock	Register in transfer-on-death (beneficiary) form, naming a custodian to manage the stock if beneficiaries are still minors when they inherit.
Mutual funds	Register in transfer-on-death (beneficiary) form.
Stamp collection, family china	Transfer by living trust.
Car	Put into joint tenancy ownership with son.
Everything else (household belongings)	Pass under will (should qualify for special "small estate" transfer procedure).

Maria adds up the value of all her property. Because it doesn't come close to the estate tax exemption amount, she doesn't expect that her children will have to pay estate tax after her death, and she doesn't need to look into methods of reducing the tax bill.

Mike: Midlife Concerns

Mike is a divorced father who owns a mortgaged house in Wyoming, a growing retirement account, and some other investments. His son, Bryce, is a teenager.

Mike, who is a healthy 50, expects quite reasonably that he will live many more years. But he is by nature a cautious person and wants to make sure that if anything happened to him, his son would be taken care of. And he hates the idea of having 5% of the value of his estate go toward probate costs and fees, when it could go for Bryce's college education instead.

The house. Mike's most valuable asset is his house. It's worth about $200,000; his equity is about $100,000. He considers making a living trust to avoid probate, but is reluctant; after all, he probably won't even own this house in 25 years' time, when death will be closer. He is delighted to find that under Wyoming law, simplified probate is available for real estate if the entire estate is valued at $200,000 or less. So, if the unexpected does happen, probate shouldn't be onerous—his executor should only have to file a few papers. He crosses the house off his list.

Retirement plan funds. This one is easy, too. Mike has named his son, Bryce, as beneficiary of his 401(k) retirement plan. But because Bryce is still younger than 18, Mike has named his ex-wife to be the custodian of the money, under the Wyoming Uniform Transfers to Minors Act. Although he doesn't want to live with her, he trusts her to use the money for the boy they both love. Under the Wyoming law, the money—whatever is left of it—must be turned over to his son when he turns 21.

Bank accounts. Mike decides it can't hurt to make his bank accounts payable on death to Bryce, again with his former wife as custodian of the funds. To do this, he just fills out and signs the form the bank teller hands him, naming Bryce as the POD payee. He knows that Bryce won't have any claim to the money now, but will receive it when Mike dies.

He follows essentially the same procedure to put his mutual fund accounts in transfer-on-death form, with Bryce as the beneficiary. He can do so because Wyoming has adopted the Uniform Transfer-on-Death Security Registration Act. (See Chapter 3.)

The car. Mike owns a nice car, one that's still worth a fair amount of money though it's three years old. But even a man of his pronounced cautiousness is sure that he will be around long after the car is rusting and abandoned. He decides not to worry about planning to avoid probate of the car.

Life insurance. Mike's main estate planning concern, at this stage of his life, isn't actually probate avoidance: It's making sure that if he died prematurely, his son would be provided for through college. So he also buys some term life insurance, naming Bryce as beneficiary, to replace the income he would have used to support Bryce. Because a life insurance policy is a contract between company and customer, the company pays the proceeds directly to the beneficiary, without probate.

Leftovers. Finally, Mike makes a simple will. He leaves everything to his son except for some small gifts to charity. He also names his sister as Bryce's personal guardian, who would look after his son in the extremely unlikely event that both Mike and his ex-wife died before Bryce reached 18. Although the items left by the will would have to go through probate, Mike realizes that this probably isn't the last will he'll make; he's using it more as a backup device than a definitive plan. If he later acquires more valuable property, setting up a probate-avoidance living trust may become justified.

Mike's Probate-Avoidance Plan	
Asset	**Plan**
House	Pass by simplified probate.
401(k) plan	Name beneficiary on form provided by plan administrator.
Bank accounts	Name payable-on-death beneficiary.
Mutual funds	Put in transfer-on-death registration.
Car	Leave by will (doesn't avoid probate).
Everything else (household belongings)	Leave by will (doesn't avoid probate).

Jim and Terry: An Unmarried Couple

Estate planning is a bigger concern to Jim and Terry than it is to most other men in their 40s. That's because Jim and Terry are a gay couple, who've been together many years and live in a state that doesn't recognize same-sex marriages. Unlike a surviving spouse, in most states, the surviving member of an unmarried couple does not have any rights to any of the deceased partner's property. (Only states that allow domestic partnerships or civil unions for same-sex partners allow a surviving unmarried partner to inherit from a deceased partner just as a spouse would, if there is no will.) In the absence of an estate plan, Jim and Terry's closest relatives would inherit their property.

They own two large assets together: their house, which is worth about $375,000, and a mutual fund account. Over the years, they've bought a television, computer, stereo, furniture, and other household items together, too. Each separately owns bank accounts, a car, and a retirement account.

Because they're in good health and relatively young, Jim and Terry don't want to invest a lot of effort in probate avoidance right now. They've been planning just to write basic wills, to be sure that property goes to the surviving partner. But first, they decide to consider some simple probate-avoidance steps—ones that won't take a lot of money or time.

The house. They start by checking the deed to their house—something they haven't looked at since they closed escrow four years ago. They find that the deed lists them as "tenants in common." That means that if one of them died tomorrow, the survivor would not automatically inherit the deceased partner's half-interest.

To solve this problem, they decide to put title to the house into joint tenancy. That way, when one partner dies, the house will automatically belong to the other. And they kill another bird with the same stone: Probate won't be required, either. All they have to do is prepare and sign a new deed, transferring the property from themselves as tenants in common to themselves as "joint tenants with right of survivorship." They record (file) the deed with the county land records office, and they're done.

That takes care of probate at the death of the first partner—but not the second. But Jim and Terry decide that they're just not willing to worry about that now. There should be plenty of time for the survivor to deal with that issue—perhaps by creating a living trust or using a transfer-on-death deed—later.

The mutual fund account. Neither Jim nor Terry can remember how they set up ownership to the mutual fund account they opened together. But when they check their latest account statement, they get a pleasant surprise: They are already joint tenants with right of survivorship—or, as the statement has it, "JT WROS." Nothing to do there.

Bank and retirement accounts. Jim and Terry decide to name each other as the payable-on-death beneficiary of the bank accounts they each own separately. It's easy and free, and again solves two problems: getting the money to the person they want to inherit it and avoiding probate. They do the same thing with their retirement accounts: On the forms provided by the account custodian, they list each other as beneficiary.

Cars, household items, and the like. Jim and Terry deal with the rest of their belongings in their wills. Each leaves his share of household items to the other, and they both also use their wills to leave gifts to family members, friends, and charities.

Those beneficiaries will probably be able to claim their property with a simple affidavit (sworn statement), without any probate court involvement. That's because Jim and Terry live in a state that offers a simple, out-of-court procedure for claiming assets when an estate contains property worth less than $50,000. Many assets—those owned in joint tenancy or held in a living trust, for example—aren't considered when determining whether or not an estate is under the $50,000 cutoff, so the estate of Jim or Terry would probably qualify for the affidavit procedure.

Jim and Terry's Probate-Avoidance Plan	
Asset	Plan
House	Put in joint tenancy.
Bank and retirement accounts	Name payable-on-death beneficiaries.
Mutual fund	Keep in joint tenancy.
Cars and everything else	Pass under wills (will probably avoid probate because of state rules for small estates).

Esther and Mark: New Love, Old Money

Esther and Mark met when they were both convinced that they would spend the rest of their lives alone. Esther had divorced after a long marriage; Mark was a widower. But their friendship grew until they realized it wasn't just friendship, it was love. They were married soon after and moved into Esther's home in Connecticut.

Esther has considerable property of her own: the house, which is worth $1 million, stocks and CDs worth another million, and valuable household furnishings. Mark is also quite comfortable financially, with his own small business and considerable savings. He has one grown son from his first marriage. Mark and Esther have kept their property separate for the sake of simplicity.

Esther wants her property, much of which she inherited from her parents, to go to her three daughters. But she doesn't want Mark to think that she's trying to cut him out, and she would want him to keep on living in her house for as long as he wished to after her death. Difficult as it is to talk about these issues, she raises them to Mark. She's immensely relieved to find that he would prefer that she leave her wealth directly to her children, with whom he gets along well. As her husband, he would have the legal right, after her death, to claim a portion of her estate.

Esther's house and other valuable items. Esther wants to give Mark the right to live in the house for the rest of his life, but have her daughters inherit it after his death. A simple probate-avoidance living trust can't do that; she needs a more complicated trust, that gives Mark the use of the property for life, after which the children inherit the property. She'll use the trust to transfer other valuable and not-so-valuable items, too, such as household furnishings and art. Another important benefit of this kind of trust is that it can save on estate taxes, which Esther's estate may owe, depending on the tax laws in effect when she dies. She'll need to see a lawyer to get the trust drawn up.

Esther's stock and bank accounts. Esther calls her stockbroker and asks about the procedure for naming her children as TOD beneficiaries for her stocks, so they can inherit them without probate. The broker sends her the paperwork. She also fills out a form provided by her bank to name them as POD payees for her CDs and other accounts.

Mark's business. Mark wants his son, David, to inherit the family business, a camera store. David already works with Mark managing the business. Mark decides that for the time being, a probate-avoidance living trust is the way to go. He transfers the business assets to a trust, naming David as the beneficiary and successor trustee.

Mark's investments. Mark wants to leave much of his other wealth, in the form of stocks and bonds, to several charities. To avoid probate for these assets, he could name the charities as transfer-on-death beneficiaries of his securities. But because his estate could be large enough to owe estate taxes, Mark plans to talk to the charities about setting up charitable trusts. Such trusts would provide income tax breaks for him while he's alive, and leave more for the charities after his death. The charities will be more than happy to discuss these plans with him.

Esther and Mark's Probate-Avoidance Plan	
Asset	**Plan**
Esther's house	Put in living trust that will avoid both probate and estate tax and to give Mark rights after Esther's death.
Esther's bank and stock accounts	Name her daughters as payable-on-death beneficiaries.
Esther's leftovers	Leave by will (won't avoid probate).
Mark's small business	Put in living trust to avoid probate (and explore other techniques to avoid estate taxes).
Mark's securities	Name charities as payable-on-death beneficiaries (and explore setting up charitable trusts to save on estate taxes).
Mark's leftovers	Leave by will (won't avoid probate).

> **RESOURCE**
>
> **More about trusts and taxes.** For more information on trusts and other ways to save on estate taxes, see *Plan Your Estate*, by Denis Clifford (Nolo).

Linda and Tomas: Comfortable

Linda and Tomas are a couple in their early 60s with what they think of as a comfortable but far from lavish lifestyle. They bought their home in a California suburb 25 years ago, and it has gone up in value far beyond what they ever expected. They've also managed to amass some savings, which they are depleting to help their two children through college and graduate school. Linda and Tomas have also contributed to company-sponsored retirement plans for many years.

They've never thought much about estate planning. But recently a friend near their age contracted a serious disease, and it got them thinking: Why not take some simple steps that will make things easier on the survivor when one of them eventually dies?

The house. Checking their deed, they find that it lists them as owners of their house "as husband and wife." A little investigating reveals that this wording means that title to the house is held as community property. A little more research, and they learn that in California, they can hold the house "in community property with right of survivorship," giving the survivor automatic ownership of the house. They decide to sign and record a new deed, changing the way they hold title. Later, after one spouse dies, the survivor will be able to create a simple probate-avoidance trust and transfer the house to it. A more cautious couple, concerned about the possibility of simultaneous death, might go ahead and make a trust now, but Linda and Tomas just don't want to bother.

The savings. Linda and Tomas hold their bank and securities accounts in joint tenancy. That means that they don't need to worry about probate when the first spouse dies. Still, they decide to convert the accounts to payable-on-death accounts, so that they can name their son and daughter to inherit after both of them have died. It's easy and doesn't cost anything, and would take effect if they both died at the same time in an accident.

The retirement accounts. Linda and Tomas have already named each other as the primary beneficiary of their retirement accounts. As alternate beneficiaries, they named their children.

Their cars. Linda and Tomas expect to outlive their current vehicles by many years. But after learning that California allows transfer-on-death car registration, they decide to register their next car that way. It's free and simple; all they do is specify the transfer-on-death owner when they register the car.

The leftovers. Linda and Tomas both write simple wills, leaving each other their other items of property. Later, if they amass lots more property, they may make a simple probate-avoidance trust. Because California has a simple small estate procedure, which currently covers estates of up to $150,000, they may decide they don't need a living trust.

Linda and Tomas's Probate-Avoidance Plan	
Asset	**Plan**
House	Hold as community property with right of survivorship, so it will automatically go to the survivor at the first spouse's death.
Bank accounts	Keep in joint tenancy; also name payable-on-death beneficiaries to inherit the funds after both parents have died.
Retirement accounts	No action needed; both Linda and Tomas have already named each other as beneficiaries, on a form provided by the plan administrators.
Cars	Register in transfer-on-death form.
Everything else (household belongings)	Leave to each other, with children as alternates, by will. (May not avoid probate; depends on value at the time of death.)

Glossary

For many more definitions of legal terms, see Nolo's free Plain-English Law Dictionary at www.nolo.com.

Administrator: The person who is appointed by the probate court, when there is no will, to collect assets of the estate, pay its debts, and distribute the rest to the beneficiaries.

Affiant: Someone who signs an affidavit.

Affidavit: A written statement of facts that is signed under oath before a notary public.

Ancillary probate: A probate proceeding conducted in a different state from the one the deceased person resided in at the time of death. Usually, ancillary probate proceedings are necessary if the deceased person owned real estate in another state.

Appraiser: A person who is hired to determine the market value of real estate or other property. A probate court sometimes appoints an appraiser to place a value on the property in an estate.

Appreciated property: Property that has gone up in value since you acquired it.

Basis: See *Tax basis*.

Beneficiary: A person or an organization who inherits property under the terms of a will, trust, or life insurance policy.

Beneficiary deed: See *Transfer-on-death deed*.

Bequeath: A legal term sometimes used in wills that means "leave"—for example, "I bequeath my diamond brooch to my daughter, Elizabeth Jenkins."

Bequest: The legal term for personal property (that's anything but real estate) left in a will.

Bond: A kind of insurance policy for executors, trustees, and guardians, who are in charge of other people's money. If they wrongfully deprive a beneficiary of property, the bonding company will replace it, up to the limits of the bond. These days, most wills state that the executor does not have to post a bond.

Charitable remainder trust: A kind of trust that allows you to make a gift to a charity during your life and get in return both annual income and, after your death, estate tax savings.

Codicil: A supplement or addition to a will. Because a codicil changes a will, it must be signed in front of witnesses, just like a will.

Community property: Ten states (listed in Chapter 6) follow a system of law called community property. In those states, very generally, all property acquired by a couple while married is community property, except for gifts to and inheritances by one spouse only, or unless the spouses have signed an agreement to the contrary. If separate property and community property are mixed together (commingled) in a bank account and expenditures made from the account, the goods purchased are usually treated as community property unless they can be specifically linked to separate property.

Community property with right of survivorship: A special way for married couples to hold title to property, available in some community property states. It allows one spouse's half-interest in community property to pass to the surviving spouse without probate.

Costs of administration: Costs of taking a probate proceeding through court, including such expenses as probate court filing fees, attorneys' fees, accountant fees, appraisers' fees, bond premiums, and fees for public notices.

Creditor: For probate purposes, a creditor is any person or entity to whom a deceased person was liable for money at the time of death.

Custodian: Someone authorized to manage property given to or inherited by a child, under laws called the Uniform Transfers to Minors Act or the Uniform Gifts to Minors Act.

Decedent: Someone who has died.

Decree: A court order.

Deed: A document that transfers ownership of a piece of real estate. There are many types of deeds that may be used for different kinds of transfers.

Deed of trust: A special type of deed similar to a mortgage.

Devise: An old legal term that is generally used to refer to real estate left under a will. In some states, the term now applies to any kind of property left by will.

Devisee: A person or entity who inherits real estate under the terms of a will.

Distributees: Another term for heirs and beneficiaries, or the people who inherit a deceased person's assets.

Donee: Someone who receives a gift.

Donor: Someone who gives a gift.

Encumbrances: Debts (for example, mortgages, property taxes, mechanic's liens, judgment liens, deeds of trust, security interests) tied to specific property as collateral.

Equity: The difference between the fair market value of your real estate and personal property and the amount you still owe on it, if any.

Escheat: The legal doctrine under which property belonging to a deceased person with no heirs passes to the state.

Estate: Generally, the property you own when you die. There are different kinds of estates, including your taxable estate (what is subject to tax), your probate estate (what must go through probate), and your net estate (your net worth).

Estate planning: Taking steps, while you're alive, to leave your property to your loved ones with a minimum of fuss, expense, and taxes.

Estate taxes: See *Federal gift and estate tax.*

Executor: The person specified in a will to manage the estate, deal with the probate court, and collect and distribute assets as the will has specified. If there is no will, or no executor nominated under the will, the probate court will appoint such a person, who is usually called the "administrator" of the estate.

Executrix: A term, now rarely used, for a female executor.

Fair market value: That price for which an item of property would be purchased by a willing buyer and sold by a willing seller. All estates are appraised for their fair market value. The result determines whether they qualify for small estate procedures and whether estate taxes are due.

Family allowance: A certain amount of a deceased person's money to which immediate family members are entitled when probate proceedings are begun. The amount is determined by state law and varies greatly from state to state.

Federal gift and estate tax: A tax imposed by the federal government on people who give away or leave large amounts of property.

Gift: Property passed to another for nothing in return or for substantially less than its actual market value. Any gift of more than a certain amount per year to an individual requires a gift tax return and may be subject to the federal gift tax.

Grantor: Someone who creates a trust. Also called trustor or settlor.

Gross estate: For federal estate tax filing purposes, the total of all property you own at death, without regard to any debts or liens against the property or the costs of administering the estate. However, taxes are due only on the value of the property the person actually owned. In some states, the gross estate is used when computing attorneys' fees for probating estates; the lawyer gets a percentage of the gross estate.

Heir: Generally, any person who is entitled by law to inherit if an estate is not completely disposed of under a will or another method of leaving property at death.

Holographic will: An unwitnessed will in which the signature and all significant provisions are in the handwriting of the person making it. Holographic wills are valid in about half the states.

Inheritance tax: A tax imposed by some states on property owned by a deceased person.

Intangible personal property: Property that does not have a physical form but is represented by a document. Stock in a corporation, the right to receive a pension, patents, and copyrights are all examples of intangible personal property.

Inter vivos trust: See *Living trust.*

Intestate: Someone who dies without having made a valid will is said to die "intestate." In that event, the estate is distributed according to the laws governing intestate succession.

Intestate succession: The method by which property is distributed when a person fails to leave a valid will. Each state's law provides that the property be distributed to the closest surviving relatives. The intestate succession laws of the various states are similar, but not identical. In most states, the surviving spouse, children, parents, siblings, nieces and nephews, and next of kin, inherit in that order.

Inventory: A complete listing of all property owned by a deceased person at death. It is filed with the probate court if probate proceedings are begun.

Issue: A term generally meaning all your children and their children down through the generations: grandchildren, great-grandchildren, and so on. A term often used in place of issue is "lineal descendants."

Joint tenancy: A way to hold title to jointly owned real estate or other property. When two or more people own property as joint tenants, and one of them dies, the others automatically become owners of the deceased owner's share. Because of this "right of survivorship," a joint tenancy interest in property does not go through probate.

Legacy: An old legal word meaning a transfer of personal property by will. The more common term for this type of transfer is bequest.

Letters of administration: A document issued by the probate court that appoints someone as the administrator of an estate.

Letters testamentary: The document given to an executor by the probate court, authorizing the executor to settle the estate.

Lien: A legal claim against your property.

Lineal descendants: See *Issue.*

Living trust: A probate-avoidance trust you create while you're alive and that remains under your control. At your death, property held in trust passes directly to the trust beneficiaries, free of probate. Also called "inter vivos" (Latin for "among the living") trusts.

Marital exemption: A deduction allowed by the federal estate tax laws for all property passed to a surviving spouse who is a U.S. citizen. This deduction (which really acts like an exemption) allows anyone, even a billionaire, to pass his entire estate to a surviving spouse without any tax at all.

Marital property: A term used in Wisconsin for certain property owned by a married couple; for practical purposes, it is the Wisconsin version of "community property."

Minor: In almost every state, any person younger than 18 years of age.

Net estate: The value of all property owned at death less liabilities.

Next of kin: The closest relatives (as defined by state law) of a deceased person.

Notary public: Someone authorized by state law to witness signatures on legal documents and sign them as evidence of the signature's validity.

Payable-on-death account: A bank account for which you have named a beneficiary (called a POD payee). The payee has no rights while you are alive but will inherit the funds in the account without probate when you die.

Personal property: Any kind of property except real estate.

Personal representative: A generic title applied to an administrator or executor of an estate. Some states use this term instead of executor or administrator.

Petition: Any document filed with a court requesting a court order. In the probate context, the term normally describes the initial document filed with the probate court requesting that the estate be "probated," subsequent requests by the executor for permission to take certain actions, and a final request to discharge the executor or administrator and close the estate.

Pretermitted (omitted) heir: A child or spouse who is not mentioned in a will and who a court believes was accidentally overlooked by the person who made the will—typically, when a child is born or adopted after the will is made. If the court determines that an heir was pretermitted, that heir is entitled to receive the same share of the estate as he or she would have had the testator died intestate.

Probate: Generally, the process by which: 1) The authenticity of your will, if any, is established, 2) your executor or administrator is appointed, 3) your debts and taxes are paid, 4) your heirs are identified, and 5) property in your probate estate is distributed according to your will or state intestate succession laws.

Probate estate: All the assets owned at death that require some form of court proceeding before title may be transferred to the heirs. Property that passes automatically at death (property in a trust, life insurance proceeds, or property held in joint tenancy, for example) is not part of the probate estate.

Quasi-community property: If a married couple moves to a community property state, certain property they acquired in their previous home may be considered "quasi-community property." The rules vary from state to state. Quasi-community property is treated just like community property.

Real property: Another term for real estate. It includes land, of course, and things attached to the land such as trees and crops, buildings, and stationary mobile homes. Anything that is not real property is termed personal property. See *Personal property.*

Residence: The place a person considers and treats as home. For example, although senators typically spend most of their time in Washington, DC, they generally consider the states they come from as their legal residences. With rare exceptions, a person may have only one residence. A deceased person's estate, with the exception of certain property located in other states, is subject to the laws of the state where the person resided at the time of death.

Residuary estate: All the property in the probate estate except for property that is specifically and effectively left to designated beneficiaries.

Securities: Stocks and bonds.

Separate property: In community property states, all property owned by a married person that is not community or quasi-community property. Separate property generally includes all property acquired before the marriage or after a legal separation, property acquired by separate gift or inheritance at any time, property acquired from separate property funds, and property that has been designated separate property by agreement of the spouses.

Succession: Inheriting property under your state's intestate succession law instead of a will.

Successor trustee: The person named in a trust document to take over as trustee after the death or incapacity of the original trustee. With a probate-avoidance living trust, the successor trustee's main job is to distribute trust assets after the original trustee's death.

Summary probate: A relatively simple probate proceeding available to "small estates" as that term is defined by state law. (Every state's definition is different.)

Surviving spouse: A widow or widower.

Tangible personal property: Personal property that takes a tangible form, such as automobiles, furniture, and heirlooms. Although such items as stock ownership and copyrights may be represented by paper certificates, the actual property is considered intangible. See *Intangible personal property.*

Tax basis: The figure used to calculate taxable gain or loss when you sell an item of property. Generally, the amount of your basis is what you paid for the item, or if you inherited it, its market value at the time you acquired it. If you have a basis of $100, and sell the item for $300, you have a taxable gain of $200.

Taxable estate: Property subject to the federal gift and estate tax. It's the fair market value of all assets owned at death (gross estate) less certain allowable deductions, such as debts, last illness and funeral expenses, and expenses of administering the estate.

Tenancy by the entirety: A special kind of joint tenancy that's only for married couples and, in states that allow this, to same-sex couples who have registered with the state. It is available in about half the states.

Tenancy in common: A way two or more people can own property together. Each can leave his or her interest upon death to beneficiaries of his or her choosing instead of to the other owners (as is the case with joint tenancy). Also, unlike joint tenancy in most states, the ownership shares need not be equal.

Testate: Someone who dies after making a valid will is said to have died "testate."

Testator: A person who makes a will.

Transfer agent: A representative of a corporation who is authorized to transfer ownership of the corporation's stock from one person to another.

Transfer-on-death deed: A deed, allowed in several states, that takes effect only at the property owner's death. It's a way to leave real estate without probate. Also called beneficiary deed.

Trust: An arrangement under which one person, called the trustee, holds legal title to property on behalf of another, called the beneficiary. See *Living trust.*

Trustee: The person who has legal authority over assets held in trust. With a simple probate-avoidance trust, the person who creates the trust is also the trustee.

Uniform Gifts to Minors Act: A set of statutes adopted by many states that allows you to appoint a custodian to manage certain kinds of property you give to a minor during your life.

Uniform Transfer-on-Death Securities Registration Act: A statute adopted by most states that allows you to name a beneficiary to inherit your stocks or bonds without probate.

Uniform Transfers to Minors Act: A set of statutes adopted by most states that provides a way for someone to give or leave property to a minor by appointing a "custodian" to manage the property for the minor.

Will: A document, signed and witnessed as required by law, in which you state whom you want to inherit your property and name a guardian to raise your young children if it's necessary.

State Information

Alabama 221

Alaska 222

Arizona 223

Arkansas 224

California 225

Colorado 227

Connecticut 228

Delaware 229

District of Columbia 230

Florida 231

Georgia 232

Hawaii 233

Idaho 234

Illinois 235

Indiana 236

Iowa 237

Kansas 238

Kentucky 239

Maine 240

Maryland 241

Massachusetts 242

Michigan 243

Minnesota 244

Mississippi 245

Missouri 246

Montana 247

Nebraska 248

Nevada 249

New Hampshire 250

New Jersey 251

New Mexico 252

New York 253

North Carolina 254

North Dakota 255

Ohio 256

Oklahoma 257

Oregon 258

Pennsylvania 259

Rhode Island 260

South Carolina 261

South Dakota 262

Tennessee 263

Texas 264

Utah 265

Vermont 266

Virginia 267

Washington 268

West Virginia 270

Wisconsin 271

Wyoming 272

Here are summaries of some rules that apply in your state. When you look up information for your state, please keep two important things in mind:

- **These are only summaries of state laws.** Citations to the laws are included so that you can look up and read them yourself. They may contain details that are critical in your situation.
- **Laws change.** Before you rely on the information here, make sure it hasn't changed since this book was printed. To take just one example, states frequently redefine what they consider a "small estate" that's eligible for probate shortcuts.

Alabama

Topic	State Rule
Uniform Transfers to Minors Act	If custodian appointed in will or trust, custodianship ends at age 21. Ala. Code §§ 35-5A-1 and following
Transfer-on-death registration for securities	Yes
Transfer-on-death registration for vehicles	No
Transfer-on-death deeds for real estate	No
Tenancy by the entirety	No
Community property	No
Affidavit procedure for small estates	No
Summary probate for small estates	Available to surviving spouse or to other inheritors if there is no real estate. Estate's value cannot exceed $25,000 (adjusted annually for inflation). 30-day waiting period. Ala. Code §§ 43-2-690 and following
Uniform Probate Code	No

Alaska

Topic	State Rule
Uniform Transfers to Minors Act	If custodian appointed in will or trust, custodianship ends at age 18 to 25. Alaska Stat. §§ 13.46.010 and following
Transfer-on-death registration for securities	Yes
Transfer-on-death registration for vehicles	No
Transfer-on-death deeds for real estate	No
Tenancy by the entirety	Yes, for real estate only.
Community property	Yes, if married couples sign an agreement making their property community property. Alaska Stat. §§ 34.77.030, 34.77.090
Survivorship community property	Yes. Alaska Stat. § 34.77.110(e)
Affidavit procedure for small estates	Estates of up to $15,000, less liens and encumbrances; 30-day waiting period. Alaska Stat. § 13.16.680
Summary probate for small estates	Value of entire estate, less liens and encumbrances, does not exceed homestead allowance, exempt property, family allowance, costs and expenses of administration, funeral expenses, and medical and hospital expenses of the last illness. Alaska Stat. §§ 13.16.690, 695
Uniform Probate Code	Yes

Arizona

Topic	State Rule
Uniform Transfers to Minors Act	If custodian appointed in will or trust, custodianship ends at age 21. Ariz. Rev. Stat. §§ 14-7651 to 13.46.195
Transfer-on-death registration for securities	Yes
Transfer-on-death registration for vehicles	Yes, but subject to limit on personal property that applies to affidavit procedure (below). Ariz. Rev. Stat. Ann. § 28-2055
Transfer-on-death deeds for real estate	Yes. Ariz. Rev. Stat. Ann. § 33-405
Tenancy by the entirety	No
Community property	Yes
Survivorship community property	Yes. Ariz. Rev. Stat. § 33-431
Affidavit procedure for small estates	1. Value of all personal property in estate, less liens and encumbrances, is $75,000 or less. 30-day waiting period. Ariz. Rev. Stat. Ann. § 14-3971.B 2. Value of all Arizona real property in the estate, less liens and encumbrances, is $100,000 or less at the date of death, and all debts and taxes have been paid. Ariz. Rev. Stat. Ann. § 14-3971.E
Summary probate for small estates	Value of entire estate, less liens and encumbrances, does not exceed allowance in lieu of homestead, exempt property, family allowance, costs of administration, funeral expenses, and expenses of the last illness. Six-month waiting period. Ariz. Rev. Stat. Ann. §§ 14-3973, 3974
Uniform Probate Code	Yes

Arkansas

Topic	State Rule
Uniform Transfers to Minors Act	If custodian appointed in will or trust, custodianship ends at age 18–21. Ark. Code Ann. §§ 9-26-201 and following
Transfer-on-death registration for securities	Yes
Transfer-on-death registration for vehicles	Yes. Ark. Code Ann. § 27-14-727
Transfer-on-death deeds for real estate	Yes. Ark. Code Ann. § 18-12-608
Tenancy by the entirety	Yes
Community property	No
Affidavit procedure for small estates	None
Summary probate for small estates	1. Personal property does not exceed that to which the widow, if any, or minor children, if any, are by law entitled free of debt, as dower or curtesy and statutory allowances. Probate court can order entire estate to surviving spouse and/or minor children. Ark. Code Ann. § 28-41-103 2. Value, less encumbrances, of all property owned by the deceased person, excluding the homestead of and the statutory allowances for the benefit of a spouse or minor children, if any, does not exceed $50,000. 45-day waiting period. Ark. Code Ann. § 28-41-101
Uniform Probate Code	No

California

Topic	State Rule
Uniform Transfers to Minors Act	If custodian appointed in will or trust, custodianship ends at age 18–25. Cal. Prob. Code §§ 3900 and following
Transfer-on-death registration for securities	Yes
Transfer-on-death registration for vehicles	Yes. Cal. Veh. Code § 4150.7
Transfer-on-death deeds for real estate	No
Tenancy by the entirety	No
Community property	Yes
Survivorship community property	Yes. Cal. Civ. Code § 682.2
Affidavit procedure for small estates	1. For personal property in estates up to $150,000 in value, as calculated using exclusions listed in "summary probate" section, below; 40-day waiting period. Cal. Prob. Code §§ 13050, 13100, and following 2. For real estate up to $50,000 in value. Six-month waiting period. Cal. Prob. Code §§ 13200 to 13208 3. For compensation owed to deceased person, up to $15,000 indexed for inflation); may be collected by surviving spouse. Cal Prob. Code §§ 13600, 13601

California (continued)

Topic	State Rule
Summary probate for small estates	Value up to $150,000. Excluded from calculating value: real estate outside California; joint tenancy property; property that goes outright to a surviving spouse; life insurance, death benefits, and other assets not subject to probate that pass to named beneficiaries; multiple-party accounts and payable-on-death accounts; any registered manufactured or mobile home; any numbered vessel; registered motor vehicles; salary up to $15,000; amounts due deceased person for services in the armed forces; property held in trust, including a living trust. Cal. Prob. Code §§ 13150 and following
Uniform Probate Code	No

Colorado

Topic	State Rule
Uniform Transfers to Minors Act	If custodian appointed in will or trust, custodianship ends at age 21. Colo. Rev. Stat. Ann. §§ 11-50-101 and following
Transfer-on-death registration for securities	Yes
Transfer-on-death registration for vehicles	No
Transfer-on-death deeds for real estate	Yes. Colo. Rev. Stat. § 15-15-402
Tenancy by the entirety	No
Community property	No
Affidavit procedure for small estates	Estates where fair market value of property that is subject to disposition by will or state intestate succession law, less liens and encumbrances, is $60,000 or less. (This excludes joint tenancy property, property in a living trust, payable-on-death bank accounts, and other kinds of property that don't pass under a will.) Ten-day waiting period. Colo. Rev. Stat. Ann. § 15-12-1201
Summary probate for small estates	Value of entire estate, less liens and encumbrances, does not exceed the value of personal property held by the deceased person as fiduciary or trustee, exempt property allowance, family allowance, costs of administration, funeral expenses, and medical expenses of last illness. Colo. Rev. Stat. Ann. § 15-12-1203
Uniform Probate Code	Yes

Connecticut

Topic	State Rule
Uniform Transfers to Minors Act	If custodian appointed in will or trust, custodianship ends at age 21. Conn. Gen. Stat. §§ 45a-557 and following
Transfer-on-death registration for securities	Yes
Transfer-on-death registration for vehicles	Yes Conn. Gen. Stat. Ann. § 14-16
Transfer-on-death deeds for real estate	No
Tenancy by the entirety	No
Community property	No
Affidavit procedure for small estates	No
Summary probate for small estates	No real estate (except real estate held in survivorship form), estate not exceeding $40,000 in value. Conn. Gen. Stat. § 45a-273
Uniform Probate Code	No

Delaware

Topic	State Rule
Uniform Transfers to Minors Act	If custodian appointed in will or trust, custodianship ends at age 21. Del. Code Ann. tit. 12, §§ 4501 and following
Transfer-on-death registration for securities	Yes
Transfer-on-death registration for vehicles	Yes. Del. Code Ann. tit. 21 § 2304
Transfer-on-death deeds for real estate	No
Tenancy by the entirety	Yes
Community property	No
Affidavit procedure for small estates	Estates without solely owned Delaware real estate and a value of no more than $20,000. (Jointly owned property, and death benefits that pass outside of probate, such as insurance or pension proceeds, are not counted toward the $20,000 limit.) 30-day waiting period. Available only to spouse, certain relatives, or funeral director. Del. Code Ann. tit. 12, § 2306
Summary probate for small estates	No
Uniform Probate Code	No

District of Columbia

Topic	State Rule
Uniform Transfers to Minors Act	If custodian appointed in will or trust, custodianship ends at age 18–21. D.C. Code Ann. §§ 21-301 and following
Transfer-on-death registration for securities	Yes
Transfer-on-death registration for vehicles	No
Transfer-on-death deeds for real estate	Yes. D.C. Code Ann. § 19-604
Tenancy by the entirety	Yes
Community property	No
Affidavit procedure for small estates	Deceased person owned nothing but one or two motor vehicles. D.C. Code Ann. § 20-357
Summary probate for small estates	Property subject to administration in D.C. has value of $40,000 or less. D.C. Code Ann. §§ 20-351 and following
Uniform Probate Code	No

Florida

Topic	State Rule
Uniform Transfers to Minors Act	If custodian appointed in will or trust, custodianship ends at age 21. Fla. Stat. Ann. §§ 710.101 and following
Transfer-on-death registration for securities	Yes
Transfer-on-death registration for vehicles	No
Transfer-on-death deeds for real estate	No
Tenancy by the entirety	Yes
Community property	No
Affidavit procedure for small estates	No
Summary probate for small estates	1. No real estate, and all property is exempt from creditors' claims except amounts needed to pay funeral and two months' last illness expenses. Upon letter to court, court will authorize transfer of property to people entitled to it. Fla. Stat. Ann. § 735.301 2. Value of entire estate subject to administration in Florida, less the value of property that is exempt from creditors' claims, doesn't exceed $75,000, OR the deceased person has been dead more than two years. Petition must be filed with court. Fla. Stat. Ann. §§ 735.201 and following
Uniform Probate Code	Yes

Georgia

Topic	State Rule
Uniform Transfers to Minors Act	If custodian appointed in will or trust, custodianship ends at age 21. Ga. Code Ann. §§ 44-5-110 and following
Transfer-on-death registration for securities	Yes
Transfer-on-death registration for vehicles	No
Transfer-on-death deeds for real estate	No
Tenancy by the entirety	No
Community property	No
Affidavit procedure for small estates	No
Summary probate for small estates	There is no will, estate owes no debts, and all heirs have agreed on how to divide the property. Ga. Code Ann. §§ 53-2-40 and following
Uniform Probate Code	No

Hawaii

Topic	State Rule
Uniform Transfers to Minors Act	If custodian appointed in will or trust, custodianship ends at age 21. Haw. Rev. Stat. §§ 553A-1 and following
Transfer-on-death registration for securities	Yes
Transfer-on-death registration for vehicles	No
Transfer-on-death deeds for real estate	Yes. Haw. Rev. Stat. §§ 527-2 and following
Tenancy by the entirety	Yes
Community property	No
Affidavit procedure for small estates	Value of property deceased person owned in Hawaii is $100,000 or less. Can transfer motor vehicles this way regardless of value of estate. Haw. Rev. Stat. §§ 560:3-1201 and following
Summary probate for small estates	Value of all property deceased person owned in Hawaii doesn't exceed $100,000. Haw. Rev. Stat. §§ 560:3-1205 and following
Uniform Probate Code	Yes

Idaho

Topic	State Rule
Uniform Transfers to Minors Act	If custodian appointed in will or trust, custodianship ends at age 21. Idaho Code §§ 68-801 and following
Transfer-on-death registration for securities	Yes
Transfer-on-death registration for vehicles	No
Transfer-on-death deeds for real estate	No
Tenancy by the entirety	No
Community property	Yes
Survivorship community property	Yes. Idaho Code § 15-6-401
Affidavit procedure for small estates	Fair market value of property subject to probate, wherever located, less liens and encumbrances, is $100,000 or less. 30-day waiting period. Idaho Code §§ 15-3-1201 and following
Summary probate for small estates	1. Value of all property deceased person owned, less liens and encumbrances, doesn't exceed the homestead allowance, exempt property, family allowance, costs of administration, funeral expenses, and medical expenses of the last illness. Idaho Code §§ 15-3-1203 and following 2. A surviving spouse who inherits everything can file petition with court, which will issue a decree to that effect. Idaho Code § 15-3-1205
Uniform Probate Code	Yes

Illinois

Topic	State Rule
Uniform Transfers to Minors Act	If custodian appointed in will or trust, custodianship ends at age 21. 760 Ill. Comp. Stat. §§ 20/1 and following
Transfer-on-death registration for securities	Yes
Transfer-on-death registration for vehicles	Yes. 625 Ill. Comp. Stat. § 5/3-107
Transfer-on-death deeds for real estate	Yes. 755 Ill. Comp. Stat. §§ 27/40 and following
Tenancy by the entirety	Yes, for real estate only.
Community property	No
Affidavit procedure for small estates	Gross value of all deceased person's property that passes under a will or by state law, excluding real estate, is $100,000 or less. 755 Ill. Comp. Stat. § 5/25-1
Summary probate for small estates	Gross value of property subject to probate in Illinois does not exceed $100,000. All heirs and beneficiaries must consent in writing. 755 Ill. Comp. Stat. § 5/9-8
Uniform Probate Code	No

Indiana

Topic	State Rule
Uniform Transfers to Minors Act	If custodian appointed in will or trust, custodianship ends at age 21. Ind. Code Ann. §§ 30-2-8.5-1 and following
Transfer-on-death registration for securities	Yes
Transfer-on-death registration for vehicles	Yes. Ind. Code Ann. § 9-17-3-9
Transfer-on-death deeds for real estate	Yes. Ind. Code Ann. § 32-17-14-11
Tenancy by the entirety	Yes, for real estate only.
Community property	No
Affidavit procedure for small estates	Value of gross probate estate, less liens and encumbrances, does not exceed $50,000. 45-day waiting period. Ind. Code § 29-1-8-1
Summary probate for small estates	Value of property subject to probate does not exceed $50,000. Ind. Code Ann. §§ 29-1-8-3 and following
Uniform Probate Code	No

Iowa

Topic	State Rule
Uniform Transfers to Minors Act	If custodian appointed in will or trust, custodianship ends at age 21. Iowa Code §§ 565B.1 and following
Transfer-on-death registration for securities	Yes
Transfer-on-death registration for vehicles	No
Transfer-on-death deeds for real estate	No
Tenancy by the entirety	No
Community property	No
Affidavit procedure for small estates	No real estate (or real estate passes to spouse as joint tenant), and gross value of the deceased person's personal property that would pass by will or intestate succession is $25,000 or less. 40-day waiting period. Iowa Code § 633.356
Summary probate for small estates	Gross value of property subject to probate does not exceed $100,000. Iowa Code § 635.1
Uniform Probate Code	No

Kansas

Topic	State Rule
Uniform Transfers to Minors Act	If custodian appointed in will or trust, custodianship ends at age 21. Kan. Stat. Ann. §§ 38-1701 and following
Transfer-on-death registration for securities	Yes
Transfer-on-death registration for vehicles	Yes. Kan. Stat. Ann. § 59-3508
Transfer-on-death deeds for real estate	Yes. Kan. Stat. Ann. § 59-3501
Tenancy by the entirety	No
Community property	No
Affidavit procedure for small estates	Value of total assets subject to probate is $20,000 or less. Kan. Stat. Ann. § 59-1507b
Summary probate for small estates	Simplified estate procedure available if court approves it, based on size of estate, wishes of heirs, and other factors. Kan. Stat. Ann. §§ 59-3202 and following
Uniform Probate Code	No

Kentucky

Topic	State Rule
Uniform Transfers to Minors Act	If custodian appointed in will or trust, custodianship ends at age 18. Ky. Rev. Stat. Ann. §§ 385.012 and following
Transfer-on-death registration for securities	Yes
Transfer-on-death registration for vehicles	No
Transfer-on-death deeds for real estate	No
Tenancy by the entirety	Yes, for real estate only.
Community property	No
Affidavit procedure for small estates	No
Summary probate for small estates	No will leaves personal property, and there is a surviving spouse, and value of property subject to probate is $15,000 or less, or if there is no surviving spouse and someone else has paid at least $15,000 in preferred claims. Ky. Rev. Stat. Ann. §§ 391.030, 395.455
Uniform Probate Code	No

Maine

Topic	State Rule
Uniform Transfers to Minors Act	If custodian appointed in will or trust, custodianship ends at age 18–21. Me. Rev. Stat. Ann. tit. 33, §§ 1651 and following
Transfer-on-death registration for securities	Yes
Transfer-on-death registration for vehicles	No
Transfer-on-death deeds for real estate	No
Tenancy by the entirety	No
Community property	No
Affidavit procedure for small estates	Value of entire estate, wherever located, less liens and encumbrances, does not exceed $20,000. 30-day waiting period. Me. Rev. Stat. Ann. tit.18-A, §§ 3-1201, 1202
Summary probate for small estates	Value of entire estate, less liens and encumbrances, does not exceed homestead allowance, exempt property, family allowance, costs of administration, reasonable funeral expenses, and reasonable medical expenses of the last illness. Me. Rev. Stat. Ann. tit.18-A, § 3-1203
Uniform Probate Code	Yes

Maryland

Topic	State Rule
Uniform Transfers to Minors Act	If custodian appointed in will or trust, custodianship ends at age 21. Md. Code Ann., [Est. & Trusts] §§ 13-301 and following
Transfer-on-death registration for securities	Yes
Transfer-on-death registration for vehicles	No
Transfer-on-death deeds for real estate	No
Tenancy by the entirety	Yes
Community property	No
Affidavit procedure for small estates	No
Summary probate for small estates	Property subject to probate in Maryland has a value of $50,000 or less, or if surviving spouse is the only beneficiary, $100,000 or less. Md. Code Ann. [Est. and Trusts] §§ 5-601 and following
Uniform Probate Code	No

Massachusetts

Topic	State Rule
Uniform Transfers to Minors Act	If custodian appointed in will or trust, custodianship ends at age 21. Mass. Gen. Laws ch. 201A, §§ 1 and following
Transfer-on-death registration for securities	Yes
Transfer-on-death registration for vehicles	No
Transfer-on-death deeds for real estate	No
Tenancy by the entirety	Yes
Community property	No
Affidavit procedure for small estates	No
Summary probate for small estates	1. Estate contains no real estate and is worth no more than $25,000 plus value of vehicle. Interested person files will (if any), inventory of assets, and list of heirs with court, and offers to serve as voluntary personal representative. Mass. Gen. Laws Ann. §§ 3-1201, 1202 2. Value of entire estate, less liens and encumbrances, does not exceed exempt property, family allowance, costs of administration, funeral expenses, and expenses of the last illness. Personal representative may immediately disburse estate and file closing statement. Mass. Gen. Laws Ann. §§ 3-1203, 1204
Uniform Probate Code	Yes

Michigan

Topic	State Rule
Uniform Transfers to Minors Act	If custodian appointed in will or trust, custodianship ends at age 18–21. Mich. Comp. Laws §§ 554.521 and following
Transfer-on-death registration for securities	Yes
Transfer-on-death registration for vehicles	No
Transfer-on-death deeds for real estate	No
Tenancy by the entirety	Yes
Community property	No
Affidavit procedure for small estates	Estate does not include real estate, and value of the entire estate, less liens and encumbrances, doesn't exceed $15,000. 28-day waiting period. Mich. Comp. Laws § 700.3983
Summary probate for small estates	1. Value of gross estate, after payment of funeral and burial costs, is $15,000 or less. Court can order property turned over to surviving spouse or heirs. Mich. Comp. Laws § 700.3982 2. Value of entire estate, less liens and encumbrances, does not exceed homestead allowance, family allowance, exempt property, costs of administration, and reasonable expenses of last illness and funeral. Mich. Comp. Laws § 700.3987
Uniform Probate Code	No (but the state has adopted large parts)

Minnesota

Topic	State Rule
Uniform Transfers to Minors Act	If custodian appointed in will or trust, custodianship ends at age 21. Minn. Stat. Ann. §§ 527.21 and following
Transfer-on-death registration for securities	Yes
Transfer-on-death registration for vehicles	No
Transfer-on-death deeds for real estate	Yes. Minn. Stat. Ann. § 507.071
Tenancy by the entirety	No
Community property	No
Affidavit procedure for small estates	$20,000 limit for entire probate estate, wherever located, including any contents of a safe deposit box, less liens and encumbrances. 30-day waiting period. Minn. Stat. § 524.3-1201
Summary probate for small estates	If court determines that no property is subject to creditors' claims (because it is exempt from claims or must be set aside for the spouse and children), can order estate closed without further proceedings. Minn. Stat. Ann. § 524.3-1203
Uniform Probate Code	Yes

Mississippi

Topic	State Rule
Uniform Transfers to Minors Act	If custodian appointed in will or trust, custodianship ends at age 21. Miss. Code Ann. §§ 91-20-1 and following
Transfer-on-death registration for securities	Yes
Transfer-on-death registration for vehicles	No
Transfer-on-death deeds for real estate	No
Tenancy by the entirety	Yes
Community property	No
Affidavit procedure for small estates	For bank accounts only, up to $12,500, if there is no will. Person claiming money must sign bond guaranteeing to pay any lawful debts of the deceased to the extent of the withdrawal. Miss. Code Ann. § 81-14-383
Summary probate for small estates	Value of estate is $500 or less. Miss. Code Ann. § 91-7-147
Uniform Probate Code	No

Missouri

Topic	State Rule
Uniform Transfers to Minors Act	If custodian appointed in will or trust, custodianship ends at age 21. Mo. Rev. Stat. §§ 404.005 and following
Transfer-on-death registration for securities	Yes
Transfer-on-death registration for vehicles	Yes. Mo. Rev. Stat. § 301.681
Transfer-on-death deeds for real estate	Yes. Mo. Rev. Stat. § 461.025
Tenancy by the entirety	Yes
Community property	No
Affidavit procedure for small estates	No
Summary probate for small estates	Value of entire estate, less liens and encumbrances, is $40,000 or less. Mo. Rev. Stat. § 473.097
Uniform Probate Code	No

Montana

Topic	State Rule
Uniform Transfers to Minors Act	If custodian appointed in will or trust, custodianship ends at age 21. Mont. Code Ann. §§ 72-26-501 and following
Transfer-on-death registration for securities	Yes
Transfer-on-death registration for vehicles	No
Transfer-on-death deeds for real estate	Yes. Mont. Code Ann. § 72-6-121
Tenancy by the entirety	No
Community property	No
Affidavit procedure for small estates	Value of entire estate, wherever located, less liens and encumbrances, is $50,000 or less. 30-day waiting period. Mont. Code Ann. § 72-3-1101
Summary probate for small estates	Value of entire estate, less liens and encumbrances, doesn't exceed homestead allowance, exempt property, family allowance, costs of administration, funeral expenses, and medical expenses of the last illness. Mont. Code Ann. § 72-3-1103
Uniform Probate Code	Yes

Nebraska

Topic	State Rule
Uniform Transfers to Minors Act	If custodian appointed in will or trust, custodianship ends at age 21. Neb. Rev. Stat. §§ 43-2701 and following
Transfer-on-death registration for securities	Yes
Transfer-on-death registration for vehicles	Yes. Neb. Rev. Stat. § 30-2715.01
Transfer-on-death deeds for real estate	Yes. Neb. Rev. Stat. § 76-3401 and following
Tenancy by the entirety	No
Community property	No
Affidavit procedure for small estates	**Personal property.** Value of all personal property, wherever located, less liens and encumbrances, is $50,000 or less. 30-day waiting period. Neb. Rev. Stat. § 30-24,125 **Real estate.** Value of all real estate in state is $30,000 or less. 30-day waiting period. Neb. Rev. Stat. § 30-24,129
Summary probate for small estates	Value of entire estate, less liens and encumbrances, doesn't exceed homestead allowance, exempt property, family allowance, costs of administration, funeral expenses, and medical expenses of the last illness. Neb. Rev. Stat § 30-24,127
Uniform Probate Code	Yes

Nevada

Topic	State Rule
Uniform Transfers to Minors Act	If custodian appointed in will or trust, custodianship ends at age 18–25. Nev. Rev. Stat. Ann. §§ 167.010 and following
Transfer-on-death registration for securities	Yes
Transfer-on-death registration for vehicles	Yes. Nev. Rev. Stat. Ann. § 482.247
Transfer-on-death deeds for real estate	Yes. Nev. Rev. Stat. Ann. §§ 111.655-699
Tenancy by the entirety	No
Community property	Yes
Survivorship community property	Yes. Nev. Rev. Stat. Ann § 111.064
Affidavit procedure for small estates	No Nevada real estate, and gross value of property in Nevada doesn't exceed $20,000. Only surviving spouse, children, grandchildren, parents, or siblings can use affidavits. 40-day waiting period. Nev. Rev. Stat. Ann. § 146.080
Summary probate for small estates	1. Gross value of estate doesn't exceed $200,000, if court approves. Nev. Rev. Stat. Ann. §§ 145.020 and following 2. Gross value of estate, less encumbrances, doesn't exceed $100,000. Court can set aside all property for surviving spouse or minor children, or if there are neither, to pay debts. Nev. Rev. Stat. Ann. § 146.070
Uniform Probate Code	No

New Hampshire

Topic	State Rule
Uniform Transfers to Minors Act	If custodian appointed in will or trust, custodianship ends at age 21. N.H. Rev. Stat. Ann. § 463-A:1
Transfer-on-death registration for securities	Yes
Transfer-on-death registration for vehicles	No
Transfer-on-death deeds for real estate	No
Tenancy by the entirety	No
Community property	No
Affidavit procedure for small estates	No
Summary probate for small estates	If there is will naming the surviving spouse or, if no spouse, an only child, or if no spouse or child, a parent, as sole beneficiary and that spouse, child, or parent is appointed administrator; or if there's no will and the surviving spouse or, if no spouse, an only child, or if no spouse or child, a parent, is the sole heir and is appointed administrator. Administrator's filing (between six months and a year after the death) and probate court's approval are all that are required. N.H. Rev. Stat. Ann. § 553:32
Uniform Probate Code	No

New Jersey

Topic	State Rule
Uniform Transfers to Minors Act	If custodian appointed in will or trust, custodianship ends at age 18–21. N.J. Stat. Ann. §§ 46:38A-1 and following
Transfer-on-death registration for securities	Yes
Transfer-on-death registration for vehicles	No
Transfer-on-death deeds for real estate	No
Tenancy by the entirety	Yes
Community property	No
Affidavit procedure for small estates	No
Summary probate for small estates	Two procedures, available only if there is no valid will: 1. If value of all property doesn't exceed $10,000, surviving spouse or domestic partner is entitled to all of it without probate. N.J. Stat. Ann. § 3B:10-3 2. If value of all property doesn't exceed $5,000 and there is no surviving spouse or domestic partner, one heir, with the written consent of the others, can file affidavit with the court and receive all the assets. N.J. Stat. Ann. § 3B:10-4
Uniform Probate Code	No

New Mexico

Topic	State Rule
Uniform Transfers to Minors Act	If custodian appointed in will or trust, custodianship ends at age 21. N.M. Stat. Ann. §§ 46-7-11 and following
Transfer-on-death registration for securities	Yes
Transfer-on-death registration for vehicles	No
Transfer-on-death deeds for real estate	Yes. N.M. Stat. Ann. § 45-6-401
Tenancy by the entirety	No
Community property	Yes
Survivorship community property	No
Affidavit procedure for small estates	1. For real estate: If married couple owns principal residence, valued for property tax purposes at $500,000 or less, as community property, surviving spouse may file affidavit with county clerk if no other assets require probate. Six-month waiting period. N.M. Stat. Ann. § 45-3-1205 2. For other property: Value of entire estate, wherever located, less liens and encumbrances, is $50,000 or less. 30-day waiting period. N.M. Stat. Ann. § 45-3-1201
Summary probate for small estates	Value of entire estate, less liens and encumbrances, doesn't exceed personal property allowance, family allowance, costs of administration, funeral expenses, and medical expenses of the last illness. N.M. Stat. Ann. § 45-3-1203
Uniform Probate Code	Yes

New York

Topic	State Rule
Uniform Transfers to Minors Act	If custodian appointed in will or trust, custodianship ends at age 21. N.Y. Est. Powers & Trusts Law §§ 7-6.1 and following
Transfer-on-death registration for securities	Yes
Transfer-on-death registration for vehicles	No
Transfer-on-death deeds for real estate	No
Tenancy by the entirety	Yes, for real estate only.
Community property	No
Affidavit procedure for small estates	No
Summary probate for small estates	Property, excluding real estate and amounts that must be set aside for surviving family members, has a gross value of $20,000 or less. Forms available at www.nycourthelp.gov. N.Y. Surr. Ct. Proc. Act § 1301
Uniform Probate Code	No

North Carolina

Topic	State Rule
Uniform Transfers to Minors Act	If custodian appointed in will or trust, custodianship ends at age 18–21. N.C. Gen. Stat. §§ 33A-1 and following
Transfer-on-death registration for securities	Yes
Transfer-on-death registration for vehicles	No
Transfer-on-death deeds for real estate	No
Tenancy by the entirety	Yes, for real estate only.
Community property	No
Affidavit procedure for small estates	**If there was no will:** Value of personal property, less liens and encumbrances, is no more than $20,000 (or, if the surviving spouse is the sole heir, $30,000, not counting the spousal allowance) 30-day waiting period **If there was a will:** Value of personal property, less liens and encumbrances, is no more than $20,000 (or, if the surviving spouse is the sole heir, $30,000). 30-day waiting period. N.C. Gen. Stat. §§ 28A-25-1 and following
Summary probate for small estates	If surviving spouse inherits everything. N.C. Gen. Stat. §§ 28A-28-1 and following
Uniform Probate Code	No

North Dakota

Topic	State Rule
Uniform Transfers to Minors Act	If custodian appointed in will or trust, custodianship ends at age 21. N.D. Cent. Code §§ 47-24.1-01 and following
Transfer-on-death registration for securities	Yes
Transfer-on-death registration for vehicles	No
Transfer-on-death deeds for real estate	Yes. N. D. Cent. Code §§ 30.1-32.1-02 and following
Tenancy by the entirety	No
Community property	No
Affidavit procedure for small estates	Value of entire estate subject to probate, less liens and encumbrances, is $50,000 or less. 30-day waiting period. N.D. Cent. Code § 30.1-23-01
Summary probate for small estates	Value of the entire estate, less liens and encumbrances, does not exceed the homestead, plus exempt property, family allowance, costs of administration, funeral expenses, and medical expenses of the last illness. N.D. Cent. Code § 30.1-23-03
Uniform Probate Code	Yes

Ohio

Topic	State Rule
Uniform Transfers to Minors Act	If custodian appointed in will or trust, custodianship ends at age 18–21. Ohio Rev. Code Ann. §§ 5814.09 and following
Transfer-on-death registration for securities	Yes
Transfer-on-death registration for vehicles	Yes. Ohio Rev. Code Ann. § 2131.13
Transfer-on-death deeds for real estate	Yes, but called "designation affidavits." Ohio Rev. Code § 5302.22
Tenancy by the entirety	Yes, if created before April 4, 1985.
Community property	No
Affidavit procedure for small estates	No
Summary probate for small estates	Available if either: • value of the estate is $35,000 or less, or • surviving spouse inherits everything, either under a will or by law, and value of the estate is $100,000 or less. Ohio Rev. Code Ann. § 2113.03
Uniform Probate Code	No

Oklahoma

Topic	State Rule
Uniform Transfers to Minors Act	If custodian appointed in will or trust, custodianship ends at age 18–21. Okla. Stat. Ann. tit. 58, §§ 1201 and following
Transfer-on-death registration for securities	Yes
Transfer-on-death registration for vehicles	No
Transfer-on-death deeds for real estate	Yes. Okla. Stat. Ann. tit. 58, § 1252
Tenancy by the entirety	Yes
Community property	No
Affidavit procedure for small estates	Fair market value of estate subject to probate, less liens and encumbrances, is $20,000 or less, and debts and taxes have been paid. Ten-day waiting period. Someone who inherits a severed mineral interest may file affidavit with the county clerk. Okla. Stat. Ann. tit. 58, § 393
Summary probate for small estates	Available if value of estate is $200,000 or less, the person has been dead for more than five years, or the person resided in another state at the time of death. Okla. Stat. Ann tit. 58, § 245
Uniform Probate Code	No

Oregon

Topic	State Rule
Uniform Transfers to Minors Act	If custodian appointed in will or trust, custodianship ends at age 21–25. Or. Rev. Stat. §§ 126.805 and following
Transfer-on-death registration for securities	Yes
Transfer-on-death registration for vehicles	No
Transfer-on-death deeds for real estate	Yes. Or. Rev. Stat. § 93-975
Tenancy by the entirety	Yes, for real estate only.
Community property	No
Affidavit procedure for small estates	No
Summary probate for small estates	Fair market value of the estate is $275,000 or less, and not more than $75,000 of the estate is personal property and not more than $200,000 is real estate. 30-day waiting period. Or. Rev. Stat. §§ 114.505 and following
Uniform Probate Code	No

Pennsylvania

Topic	State Rule
Uniform Transfers to Minors Act	If custodian appointed in will or trust, custodianship ends at age 21–25. 20 Pa. Cons. Stat. Ann. §§ 5301 and following
Transfer-on-death registration for securities	Yes
Transfer-on-death registration for vehicles	No
Transfer-on-death deeds for real estate	No
Tenancy by the entirety	Yes
Community property	No
Affidavit procedure for small estates	No
Summary probate for small estates	Property (not counting real estate, certain vehicles, certain payments the family is entitled to, and funeral costs) is worth $50,000 or less. 20 Pa. Cons. Stat. Ann. § 3102
Uniform Probate Code	No

Rhode Island

Topic	State Rule
Uniform Transfers to Minors Act	If custodian appointed in will or trust, custodianship ends at age 21. R.I. Gen. Laws §§ 18-7-1 and following
Transfer-on-death registration for securities	Yes
Transfer-on-death registration for vehicles	No
Transfer-on-death deeds for real estate	No
Tenancy by the entirety	Yes, for real estate only.
Community property	No
Affidavit procedure for small estates	No
Summary probate for small estates	No real estate, and value of property that would be subject to probate (not counting tangible personal property) doesn't exceed $15,000. R.I. Gen. Laws § 33-24-1
Uniform Probate Code	No

South Carolina

Topic	State Rule
Uniform Transfers to Minors Act	No
Transfer-on-death registration for securities	Yes
Transfer-on-death registration for vehicles	No
Transfer-on-death deeds for real estate	No
Tenancy by the entirety	No
Community property	No
Affidavit procedure for small estates	Value of property passing by will or under law, less liens and encumbrances, is $25,000 or less. Probate judge must approve affidavit. 30-day waiting period. S.C. Code Ann. § 62-3-1201
Summary probate for small estates	Value of property passing by will or under law, less liens and encumbrances, is $25,000 or less (not counting exempt property, funeral expenses, and medical expenses of last illness). S.C. Code Ann. § 62-3-1203
Uniform Probate Code	Yes

South Dakota

Topic	State Rule
Uniform Transfers to Minors Act	If custodian appointed in will or trust, custodianship ends at age 18. S.D. Codified Laws Ann. §§ 55-10A-1 and following
Transfer-on-death registration for securities	Yes
Transfer-on-death registration for vehicles	No
Transfer-on-death deeds for real estate	No
Tenancy by the entirety	No
Community property	No
Affidavit procedure for small estates	Value of entire estate, less liens and encumbrances, is $50,000 or less. S.D. Codified Laws §§ 29A-3-1201 and following
Summary probate for small estates	"Informal probate" available regardless of value of estate. 30-day waiting period. S.D. Codified Laws Ann. §§ 29A-3-301 and following
Uniform Probate Code	Yes

Tennessee

Topic	State Rule
Uniform Transfers to Minors Act	If custodian appointed in will or trust, custodianship ends at age 21–25. Tenn. Code Ann. §§ 35-7-201 and following
Transfer-on-death registration for securities	Yes
Transfer-on-death registration for vehicles	No
Transfer-on-death deeds for real estate	No
Tenancy by the entirety	Yes
Community property	No
Affidavit procedure for small estates	No
Summary probate for small estates	Value of property, not counting property held jointly with right of survivorship or real estate, is $25,000 or less. Tenn. Code Ann. §§ 30-4-102 and following
Uniform Probate Code	No

Texas

Topic	State Rule
Uniform Transfers to Minors Act	If custodian appointed in will or trust, custodianship ends at age 21. Tex. Prop. Code Ann. §§ 141.001 and following
Transfer-on-death registration for securities	No
Transfer-on-death registration for vehicles	No
Transfer-on-death deeds for real estate	No
Tenancy by the entirety	No
Community property	Yes
Survivorship community property	Yes (with written agreement)
Affidavit procedure for small estates	There is no will, and value of entire estate, not including homestead and exempt property, is $50,000 or less. Probate judge must approve affidavit. Can be used to transfer homestead, but no other real estate. 30-day waiting period. Tex. Estates Code Ann. § 205.001-205.008
Summary probate for small estates	1. Value of property doesn't exceed that needed to pay family allowance and certain creditors. Tex. Estates Code Ann. § 354.001 and following 2. "Independent administration" available, regardless of value of estate, if requested in the will or all inheritors agree to it. Tex. Estates Code Ann. § 401.001 and following
Uniform Probate Code	No

Utah

Topic	State Rule
Uniform Transfers to Minors Act	If custodian appointed in will or trust, custodianship ends at age 21. Utah Code Ann. § 75-5a-101
Transfer-on-death registration for securities	Yes
Transfer-on-death registration for vehicles	No
Transfer-on-death deeds for real estate	No
Tenancy by the entirety	No
Community property	No
Affidavit procedure for small estates	Value of entire estate subject to probate, less liens and encumbrances, is $100,000 or less. May also transfer up to four boats, motor vehicles, trailers or semi-trailers if value of estate subject to probate, excluding the value of the vehicles, is $100,000 or less. 30-day waiting period. Utah Code Ann. § 75-3-1201
Summary probate for small estates	Value of entire estate, less liens and encumbrances, does not exceed the homestead allowance, exempt property, family allowance, costs of administration, funeral expenses, and medical expenses of the last illness. Utah Code Ann. § 75-3-1203
Uniform Probate Code	Yes

Vermont

Topic	State Rule
Uniform Transfers to Minors Act	No
Transfer-on-death registration for securities	Yes
Transfer-on-death registration for vehicles	Yes. Vt. Stat. Ann., tit. 23, § 2023
Transfer-on-death deeds for real estate	No
Tenancy by the entirety	Yes
Community property	No
Affidavit procedure for small estates	No
Summary probate for small estates	Deceased is survived by a spouse, civil union partner, or children and owned no real estate, and value of personal property is $10,000 or less. Vt. Stat. Ann., tit. 14, § 1902
Uniform Probate Code	No

Virginia

Topic	State Rule
Uniform Transfers to Minors Act	If custodian appointed in will or trust, custodianship ends at age 18–21. Va. Code Ann. §§ 64.2-1900 and following
Transfer-on-death registration for securities	Yes
Transfer-on-death registration for vehicles	No
Transfer-on-death deeds for real estate	Yes. Va. Code Ann. §§ 64.2.-621 and following
Tenancy by the entirety	Yes
Community property	No
Affidavit procedure for small estates	1. Entire personal probate estate $50,000 or less. Will, if any, must be filed with probate court. 60-day waiting period. Va. Code Ann. § 64.2-601 2. For real estate, if there's no will, the heirs or personal representative can record affidavit setting out names of heirs; clerk will send abstract of the affidavit to the revenue commissioner, and then real estate can be transferred. Va. Code Ann. § 64.2-510
Summary probate for small estates	No
Uniform Probate Code	No

Washington

Topic	State Rule
Uniform Transfers to Minors Act	If custodian appointed in will or trust, custodianship ends at age 21 or 25. Wash. Rev. Code Ann. §§ 11.114.010 and following
Transfer-on-death registration for securities	Yes
Transfer-on-death registration for vehicles	No
Transfer-on-death deeds for real estate	No
Tenancy by the entirety	No
Community property	Yes
Survivorship community property	No
Affidavit procedure for small estates	Value of assets subject to probate, not counting surviving spouse's community property interest, less liens and encumbrances, is $100,000 or less. 40-day waiting period. Wash. Rev. Code §§ 11.62.010 and following
Summary probate for small estates	The court may grant a request for settlement without court intervention if the estate is solvent and: • if there is a will, the personal representative it names makes the request, or • if there is no will, the surviving spouse or domestic partner makes the request, the estate consists entirely of community property, and the deceased person left no children or grandchildren from another relationship, or

Washington (continued)

Topic	State Rule
Summary probate for small estates (continued)	• the personal representative is not a creditor of the deceased person and the court determines it would be in the best interests of the beneficiaries and creditors. Wash. Rev. Code §§ 11.68.011 and following
Uniform Probate Code	No

West Virginia

Topic	State Rule
Uniform Transfers to Minors Act	If custodian appointed in will or trust, custodianship ends at age 21. W.Va. Code §§ 36-7-1 and following
Transfer-on-death registration for securities	Yes
Transfer-on-death registration for vehicles	No
Transfer-on-death deeds for real estate	No
Tenancy by the entirety	No
Community property	No
Affidavit procedure for small estates	No
Summary probate for small estates	Value of estate, not counting real estate, is $100,000 or less; or if the personal representative is the sole beneficiary of the estate; or if surviving spouse is the sole beneficiary of the estate; or if all the beneficiaries state that no disputes are likely, there are enough assets to pay debts and taxes, and the executor agrees. W. Va. Code § 44-3A-5
Uniform Probate Code	No

Wisconsin

Topic	State Rule
Uniform Transfers to Minors Act	If custodian appointed in will or trust, custodianship ends at age 21. Wis. Stat. Ann. §§ 54.850 and following
Transfer-on-death registration for securities	Yes
Transfer-on-death registration for vehicles	No
Transfer-on-death deeds for real estate	Yes. Wis. Stat. Ann. § 705.15
Tenancy by the entirety	No
Community property	Yes (called marital property)
Survivorship community property	Yes. Wis. Stat. Ann. §§ 766.58, 766.60
Affidavit procedure for small estates	Deceased person's solely owned property in Wisconsin is worth $50,000 or less. Wis. Stat. Ann. § 867.03
Summary probate for small estates	Value of estate, less mortgages and encumbrances, is $50,000 or less, and deceased person is survived by a spouse or minor children. Also available if value of estate, less mortgages and encumbrances, does not exceed costs, expenses, allowances, and claims. Wis. Stat. Ann. § 867.01
Uniform Probate Code	No

Wyoming

Topic	State Rule
Uniform Transfers to Minors Act	If custodian appointed in will or trust, custodianship ends at age 21. Wyo. Stat. §§ 34-13-114 and following
Transfer-on-death registration for securities	Yes
Transfer-on-death registration for vehicles	No
Transfer-on-death deeds for real estate	Yes. Wyo. Stat. §§ 2-18-101 and following
Tenancy by the entirety	Yes
Community property	No
Affidavit procedure for small estates	Value of entire estate, less liens and encumbrances, is $200,000 or less. Must file affidavit with county clerk. 30-day waiting period. Wyo. Stat. § 2-1-201
Summary probate for small estates	Value of entire estate, including real estate and mineral interests, is $200,000 or less. Wyo. Stat. § 2-1-205
Uniform Probate Code	No

Index

A

AB trust, 130
Affidavit, Death of Grantor, 93
Affidavit procedure, 162–165
 claiming wages, 160–161
 pros and cons, 163
 sample affidavit for claiming
  personal property, 165
 for small estates, 156
 for vehicles, 77–80
 waiting period, 163
 See also Small estates
Alabama, laws summarized, 221
Alaska
 joint tenancy rules, 108
 laws summarized, 222
Alternate beneficiaries
 for living trust, 127
 retirement accounts, 51–52
Arizona
 laws summarized, 223
 terminating right of
  survivorship, 117
 TOD vehicle registration, 72, 73
Arkansas
 laws summarized, 224
 Revocation of TOD
  (Beneficiary) Deed sample, 91

 TOD vehicle registration, 72, 73
Autos. *See* Transfer-on-death
 vehicle registration

B

Bank accounts. *See* Joint bank
 accounts; Payable-on-death bank
 accounts; Revocable living trust
Basis. *See* Tax basis rules
Beneficiaries
 bank accounts, 21–30
 FDIC coverage on POD
  accounts, 22
 government securities, 67–69
 real estate deeds, 82–93
 retirement accounts, 38–56
 securities, 58–69
 vehicles, 72–80
 See also Alternate beneficiaries;
  Death of beneficiary
Boats (small). *See* Transfer-on-
 death vehicle registration
Bonds, beneficiaries. *See* Transfer-
 on-death securities registration
Brokerage accounts, beneficiaries.
 See Transfer-on-death securities
 registration
Bypass trusts, 130

C

California
affidavit for claiming property resource, 165
community property and probate avoidance, 120, 121
laws summarized, 225–226
simplified probate resource, 168
TOD vehicle registration, 72, 73
Cars. *See* Transfer-on-death vehicle registration
Cash, living trust and, 152
Charitable remainder trust, 178
Charity. *See* Organization/ institution
Children
right to inherit, 9
See also Minor children
Child's trust, 141–142
Closely held corporations, 97, 147–148
Colorado
laws summarized, 227
TOD (Beneficiary) Deed sample, 89
Community property agreements, 117–120
states that allow, 118
Community property rules, 112–122
community property agreements, 117–120
gifts and, 181–182

inherited property, 113
IRA beneficiaries, 42–43
joint accounts and POD designation, 21
overview, 112–114
regular (no right of survivorship) property, 120–122
right of survivorship
adding, 116–117
holding title with, 114–117
terminating, 117
spouse's right to inherit, 8, 28–29
states listed, 112
TOD deeds, 87–88
TOD securities, 63–64
TOD vehicles, 74
See also State laws
Community property with no right of survivorship, 120–122
Community property with right of survivorship, 114–117
pros and cons, 115–116
states that allow, 115
Connecticut
laws summarized, 228
TOD vehicle registration, 72, 73
Conservatorship, avoiding with living trust, 132–133
Contractual wills, POD designation and, 30
Co-op apartments, 146
Cost of probate, 3–4

Court challenges, avoiding with
living trust, 130–131
Creditors' rights, 9–10
Custodian
for gifts to minors, 184–186
for trust property, 142
UTMA custodian, 23–25

D

Death of beneficiary
POD bank account, 30–31
TOD securities, 66
Death of Grantor Affidavit, 93
Death of joint owners
simultaneously, 102
Delaware
laws summarized, 229
"natural person" rule for POD
beneficiary, 27
TOD vehicle registration, 72, 73
Distributions. *See* Required
minimum distributions
District of Columbia, laws
summarized, 230
Divorce
and 401(k) plans, 41, 42
and POD accounts, 34
Divorced father of a teenager,
probate-avoidance scenario,
196–198
Durable power of attorney for
finances, 102, 105, 133

E

Employee Retirement Income
Security Act (ERISA), 42
Estate as beneficiary, retirement
accounts, 49
Estate taxes (federal). *See* Federal
taxes
Estate taxes (state). *See* State taxes

F

Family's right to inherit, 7–9
FDIC coverage, for beneficiaries
on POD accounts, 22
Federal taxes
gift tax, 173
joint tenancy property, 104
"Kiddie Tax," 186
living trust and, 152–153
probate does not avoid, 7
revocable living trust, 130
rules for gifts to minors, 185–186
TOD securities and, 61
See also Gifts
Florida
convenience bank accounts, 105
laws summarized, 231
POD beneficiaries and equal
shares, 26
401(k) plans
required minimum
distributions, 52–54
spouse waives right to inherit,
41–42

tax advantages, 39
See also Retirement accounts

G

Georgia
  laws summarized, 232
  limits on POD beneficiaries, 27
Gifts
  annual exclusion limit, 174–176
  charities, 178
  community property rules and,
    181–182
  "Kiddie Tax," 186
  medical bills, 176–177
  minor children, 183–186
  problematic gifts, 179–181
  pros and cons, 172
  to spouse, 177–178
  tax-free gifts, 174–178
  tuition bills, 176–177
  what to give, 181–183
  See also Federal taxes
Glossary of terms, 207–217
Government securities
  beneficiaries for, 67–69
  buying, 69

H

Hawaii
  affidavit procedure for vehicle, 77
  laws summarized, 233

I

Idaho
  community property and
    probate avoidance, 120
  laws summarized, 234
Illinois
  convenience bank accounts, 105
  laws summarized, 235
  TOD vehicle registration, 72,
    73
Indiana, laws summarized, 236
Individual retirement accounts.
  See Retirement accounts
Inherited IRA, 46–47
Inherited property, community
  property rules, 113
Institution. *See* Organization/
  institution
Inter vivos trust. *See* Revocable
  living trust
Intestate succession law, 144
Iowa, laws summarized, 237
IRAs
  beneficiaries in community
    property states, 42–43
  nonspouse beneficiary, 46–47
  required minimum
    distributions, 45, 47, 52–54
  spouse rolls over account, 44–45
  tax advantages, 39
  See also Retirement accounts

J

Joint bank accounts
  adding POD designation to,
    19–21
  durable POA instead of, 105
  problems with, 104–105
  title on, 98
Joint property ownership, 96–122
  alternatives to, 122
  avoiding probate, 97
  joint tenancy with right of
    survivorship, 97, 98–109
  tenancy by the entirety, 97,
    110–112
  types of title, 97
Joint securities accounts, TOD
  registration, 62–63
Joint tenancy with right of
  survivorship, 97, 98–109
  avoiding probate, 99–101
  death of both owners
    simultaneously, 102
  equal/non-equal property
    shares, 107
  gift and estate taxes, 104
  giving away property, 103
  "JT WROS," 107
  limitations of, 101–102
  pros and cons, 99
  separately owned property and
    surviving spouse, 106–107
  state laws and, 108–109
  taking title, 107

Joint vehicle ownership, 75–76
"JT WROS," 107

K

Kansas
  laws summarized, 238
  TOD vehicle registration, 72,
    73
Kentucky, laws summarized, 239
"Kiddie Tax," 186

L

Lawyers
  probate as profit center for, 6
  probate fees, 4
  simplified court procedures, 168
Life insurance, living trust and,
  150–151
Limited liability company, 148
Living trust. *See* Revocable living
  trust
LLC, 148
Loans, and gift tax, 179–180
Louisiana
  laws not covered, 9
  TOD registration for securities
    not allowed, 58, 59

M

Maine
  laws summarized, 240
  surviving spouse and vehicle
    transfer, 80

Married California couple,
probate-avoidance scenario,
204–206

Married couples. *See* Community
property rules; Spouse

Maryland, laws summarized, 241

Massachusetts, laws summarized,
242

Medicaid eligibility and TOD
deeds, 85

Medical bills, paying as a gift,
176–177

Michigan
joint tenancy rules, 108–109
laws summarized, 243
surviving spouse and vehicle
transfer, 80

Minimum distributions. *See*
Required minimum distributions

Minnesota
Affidavit for Collection of
Personal Property, 165
laws summarized, 244

Minor children
"Kiddie Tax," 186
living trust beneficiaries, 141–142
as POD beneficiaries, 23–25
retirement account beneficiaries,
47–48
tax-free gifts to, 183–186
as TOD securities beneficiary,
64–65

Mississippi, laws summarized, 245

Missouri

laws summarized, 246
TOD vehicle registration, 72,
73

Montana, laws summarized, 247

Motor vehicles. *See* Transfer-on-
death vehicle registration

Multiple beneficiaries
POD bank accounts, 25–27
retirement accounts, 48–49
TOD securities, 65–66

Mutual funds, beneficiaries. *See*
Transfer-on-death securities
registration

N

Nebraska
laws summarized, 248
TOD vehicle registration, 72,
73

Nevada
Death of Grantor Affidavit, 93
laws summarized, 249
terminating right of
survivorship, 117
TOD vehicle registration, 72,
73

New Hampshire, laws
summarized, 250

New Jersey, laws summarized, 251

New Mexico
community property and
probate avoidance, 120
laws summarized, 252

New York, laws summarized, 253

Nonspouse beneficiary
  required minimum
    distributions, 47
  for retirement account, 46–47

North Carolina, laws summarized,
  254

North Dakota, laws summarized,
  255

O

Ohio
  laws summarized, 256
  surviving spouse and vehicle
    transfer, 80
  TOD vehicle registration, 72,
    73

Oklahoma
  laws summarized, 257
  limits on POD beneficiaries, 27

Oregon
  affidavit procedure, 77–79
  joint tenancy rules, 108, 109
  laws summarized, 258

Organization/institution
  gifts to charities, 178
  as retirement account
    beneficiary, 50
  as successor trustee, 140

Out-of-state probate, 5

P

Partnership, 97, 147

Payable-on-death bank accounts,
  17–35
  beneficiaries, 21–30
  changing a designation, 32–33
  claiming the funds, 34–35
  contractual wills, 30
  contradictory will provisions, 33
  death of beneficiary, 30–31
  joint accounts and, 19–21
  property settlement agreements
    and, 34
  pros and cons, 16
  setting up, 17–19

Payable-on-death government
  securities accounts, 67–69

Pennsylvania, laws summarized,
  259

POA. *See* Durable power of
  attorney for finances

POD. *See* Payable-on-death

Power of attorney. *See* Durable
  power of attorney for finances

Probate-avoidance methods
  compared, 11–13
  when to plan for, 13–14

Probate-avoidance scenario
  divorced father of a teenager,
    196–198
  married California couple,
    204–206

newly married couple with
  separate assets, 201–204
retired, married couple, 190–192
unmarried gay couple, 198–201
widowed, older woman, 192–196
Probate procedures
  length of, 4–5
  overview, 2
  public nature of, 5
  reasons to avoid, 2–5
  reforming, 6
Property settlement agreements,
  POD accounts and, 34
Public nature of probate, 5

R

Real estate
  putting in a trust, 146–147
  See also Joint property
    ownership
Recording
  living trust, 153
  revocation of TOD deed, 90–91
  TOD deed, 88, 90, 92
Required minimum distributions
  calculating, 54–55
  IRAs and qualified plans, 45,
    47, 52–54
  retirement accounts, 52–56
  tax for not taking, 55
Resources
  affidavit for claiming property
    (California), 165

gift and estates taxes, 173
retirement, 187
retirement accounts, 56
revocable living trust, 138–139
successor trustee, 141
summary probate (California),
  168
Retired, married couple, probate-
  avoidance scenario, 190–192
Retirement accounts
  beneficiaries for, 38–52
  living trust and, 149
  pros and cons of beneficiaries,
    40
  required minimum
    distributions, 52–56
  resources, 56
  spouses and, 40–43
  tax advantages of, 39
Revocable living trust, 125–154
  adding property later, 145
  advantages of, 130–133
  amending, 153–154
  avoiding probate with, 126–130
  bank accounts, 149
  cash, 152
  creating a trust, 137–144
  estate taxes and, 130
  evaluating need for, 134–137
  life insurance, 150–151
  property transfer after your
    death, 128–130
  pros and cons, 126
  real estate, 146–147

registering the trust, 153
resources for, 138–139
as retirement account
  beneficiary, 49–50, 149
revoking, 153–154
sample, 143
securities, 151
small business interests, 147–148
taxes and record keeping,
  152–153
terminology, 137
transferring property to, 144
vehicles, 149–150
will still needed, 133–134
Revoking a living trust, 153–154
Revoking a TOD deed, 90–91
Rhode Island, laws summarized,
  260
Right of survivorship
  explained, 100
  See also Community property
    rules; Joint tenancy with right
    of survivorship
Right to inherit, 7–9
  See also Children; Spouse
Roth IRAs
  tax advantages, 39
  withdrawal rules, 53
  See also Retirement accounts

S

Securities
  living trust and, 151
  See also Transfer-on-death
    securities registration
Simplified court procedures,
  156–157, 166–169
  lawyers and, 168
  pros and cons, 166
  qualifying for, 167
  state laws, 168–169
  See also Small estates
Small business interests, putting
  in a trust, 147–148
Small estates
  qualifying as, 157–160
  types of property, 157–159
  See also Affidavit procedure;
    Simplified court procedures
Sole proprietorships, 147
South Carolina
  joint tenancy rules, 109
  laws summarized, 261
  UTMA and, 25
South Dakota, laws summarized,
  262
Spouse
  contractual wills, 30
  POD bank accounts and, 28–29
  retirement account beneficiary,
    44–46
  right to inherit, 7–8, 28–29
  tax-free gifts to, 177–178
  TOD securities, 63–64
  vehicle transfers, 80
  waive right to inherit 401(k)
    plans, 41–42

See also Community property
rules
State laws
  community property with right
  of survivorship, 115
  joint tenancy with right of
  survivorship, 108–109
  simplified court procedures,
  168–169
  summaries by state, 221–272
  tenancy by the entirety allowed,
  110
  TOD deeds, 83
  UTMA custodianship, 24
  See also Community property
  rules
State taxes, probate does not avoid,
7
Stepped up basis. *See* Tax basis rules
Stocks, beneficiaries. *See* Transfer-
on-death securities registration
Successor trustee, 128–130
  choosing, 139–141
  resource, 141
Summary probate. *See* Simplified
court procedures

T

Tax basis rules
  appreciated property, 106–107,
  182–183
  community property, 113–114

Tenancy by the entirety, 97,
110–112
  pros and cons, 111–112
  state that allow, 110
Tenancy in common, 97
Tennessee
  joint tenancy rules, 108
  laws summarized, 263
Terminating right of survivorship,
117
Texas
  convenience bank accounts, 105
  joint tenancy rules, 109
  laws summarized, 264
  TOD registration for securities
  not allowed, 58, 59
TOD. *See* Transfer-on-death
Totten trust, 17
  See also Payable-on-death bank
  accounts
Transfer-on-death real estate deed,
82–93
  beneficiaries, 87
  claiming TOD property, 92–93
  drawbacks of, 85–86
  Medicaid eligibility and, 85
  preparing the deed, 86
  procedures, 83–84
  pros and cons, 82
  recording, 88, 90
  recording a new deed, 92
  revoking, 90–91
  sale of property after death,
  85–86

sample of, 89

signing and notarizing, 87–88

states with TOD deeds, 83

transferring property before
death, 92

Transfer-on-death securities
registration, 58–69

changing, 67

claiming the securities, 67

death of beneficiary, 66

eligibility to use, 59–60

federal estate taxes and, 61

joint accounts and, 62–63

minor child as beneficiary,
64–65

multiple beneficiaries, 65–66

process for registration, 61

pros and cons, 59

spouse's rights, 63–64

when not to use, 67

Transfer-on-death vehicle
registration, 72–80

claiming the vehicle, 75

joint ownership, 75–76

pros and cons, 72

revoking, 74

states that allow, 72

Transfer taxes, for real estate, 146

Treasury bills, notes, and bonds.
See Government securities

Treasury Direct Tender package, 69

Trust. See AB trust; Bypass trusts;
Charitable remainder trust;
Child's trust; Revocable living trust

Tuition bills, paying as a gift,
176–177

U

Uniform Gifts to Minors Act,
184, 185

Uniform Probate Code, 2–3

Uniform Transfer-on-Death
Securities Registration Act, 59

Uniform Transfers to Minors Act
(UTMA)

minors as POD beneficiaries,
23–25

minors as trust beneficiaries, 142

Unmarried gay couple, probate-
avoidance scenario, 198–201

Utah

affidavit procedure for vehicle, 77

laws summarized, 265

UTMA. See Uniform Transfers to
Minors Act (UTMA)

V

Vehicles

living trust and, 149–150

nonprobate transfer procedures,
77–80

TOD registration, 72–76

Vermont

delayed release of POD funds,
35

laws summarized, 266

TOD vehicle registration, 72, 73
UTMA and, 25
Virginia, laws summarized, 267

W

Wages, claiming with an affidavit, 160–161
Washington, laws summarized, 268–269
West Virginia, laws summarized, 270

Widowed, older woman, probate-avoidance scenario, 192–196
Wills
changing or revoking POD designation, 33
contractual wills, 30
and living trust, 133–134
Wisconsin
joint tenancy rules, 108
laws summarized, 271
Wyoming, laws summarized, 272

⚖ NOLO Save 15% *off your next order*

Register your Nolo purchase, and we'll send you a
coupon for 15% off your next Nolo.com order!

Nolo.com/customer-support/productregistration

On Nolo.com you'll also find:

Books & Software

Nolo publishes hundreds of great books and software programs for consumers and
business owners. Order a copy, or download an ebook version instantly, at Nolo.com.

Online Legal Documents

You can quickly and easily make a will or living trust, form an LLC or corporation, apply
for a trademark or provisional patent, or make hundreds of other forms—online.

Free Legal Information

Thousands of articles answer common questions about everyday legal issues
including wills, bankruptcy, small business formation, divorce, patents,
employment, and much more.

Plain-English Legal Dictionary

Stumped by jargon? Look it up in America's most up-to-date source for
definitions of legal terms, free at nolo.com.

Lawyer Directory

Nolo's consumer-friendly lawyer directory provides in-depth profiles of lawyers all
over America. You'll find all the information you need to choose the right lawyer.